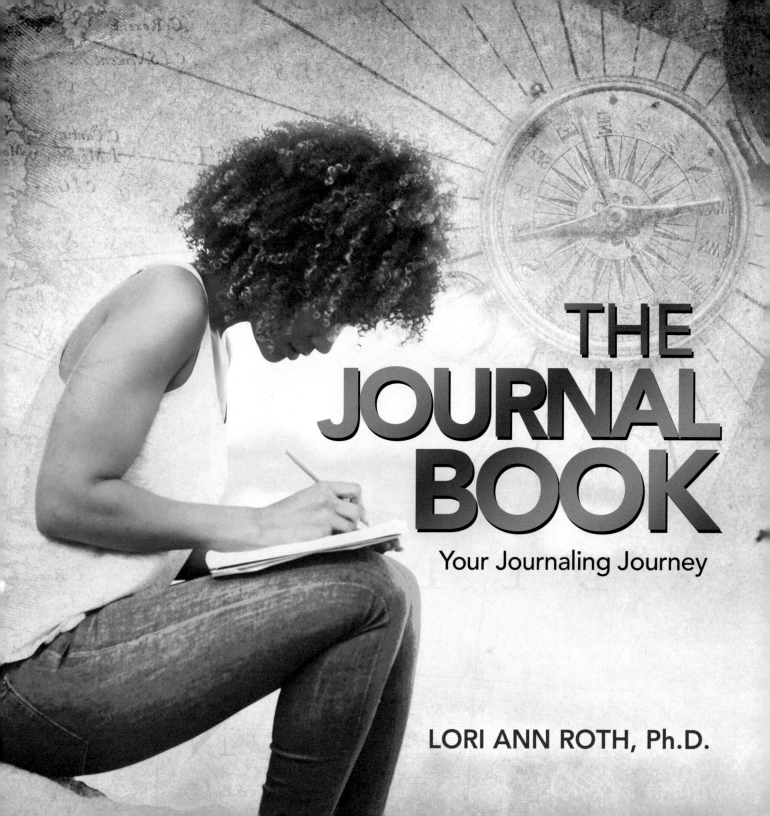

Balboa Press books may be ordered through booksellers or by contacting:

Balboa Press
A Division of Hay House
1663 Liberty Drive
Bloomington, IN 47403
www.balboapress.com
1 (877) 407-4847

Because of the dynamic nature of the Internet, any web addresses or links contained in
this book may have changed since publication and may no longer be valid. The views
expressed in this work are solely those of the author and do not necessarily reflect the views
of the publisher, and the publisher hereby disclaims any responsibility for them.

Any people depicted in stock imagery provided by Getty Images are models,
and such images are being used for illustrative purposes only.
Certain stock imagery © Getty Images.

Interior Graphics/Art Credit: Lori Ann Roth Ph.D.
Author Photo Credit: Jola Bremer of Evoke LLC

ISBN: 978-1-9822-2437-0 (sc)
ISBN: 978-1-9822-2438-7 (e)

Library of Congress Control Number: 2019903446

Print information available on the last page.
Balboa Press rev. date: 04/15/2019

Balboa
PRESS
A DIVISION OF HAY HOUSE

"Whether you're keeping a journal or writing as a meditation, it's the same thing. What's important is you're having a relationship with your mind."

Natalie Goldberg

This book is dedicated to Angel David Garcia, my supportive, and loving husband.

CONTENTS

ACKNOWLEDGEMENTS

First of all, thank you to my best friend, Carol Powers, you encouraged me when I needed the support. It always seems like I am in a good place when you are not, and vice versa. Thank you to all of my content editors who read the book and gave me helpful suggestions. Sheri Kaye Hoff, Tami Krebs, and Blake Barber, you are intelligent, creative, and so helpful. Thank you to all of the people who agreed to be interviewed and/or share their story. You all know who you are and I am so appreciative and grateful. Thank you to my editor, Liz Coursen. Liz, you are amazing.

A special thank you to Sarah Turner of Balboa Press. You guided me through this process with your knowledge, patience, and determination.

*Some names have been changed to protect the privacy of contributors.

INTRODUCTION

Life is so amazing. I am sitting on my favorite beach, near my house, watching the beautiful sunset with my husband, Angel. We are drinking wine, relaxing, and breathing the salt sea air. As I close my eyes, I begin reflecting on how I got here. What was the catalyst that drove me to sell my home I'd had for 20 years, leave my secure job, move to the beach, and start my company?... I realized that my journaling practice drove my decisions. My great transformations in my life stemmed from my journaling...I knew I needed to share this powerful process, and decided to write this book about journaling. I hope this book can help make your dreams come true too.

Have you ever written a letter but never mailed (or emailed) it to the recipient? Have you started a journal at one time but never continued writing? Are you not a great writer? Would you like to be healthier, wealthier, or maybe less stressed? Well, if you can relate to any of these things or are interested in journaling, this book is for you.

Remember that time in your life when you were so very happy? Was it that special vacation with loved ones at the lake in the mountains? Your children learning how to fish and canoeing for the first time? Was it your wedding day? Remember that feeling of joy and love and having your friends and family supporting you? Did you experience the major life achievement of finally reaching your goal? Did you get that promotion, have that wonderful family, or start that business? Don't you wish that you could go back and remember those precious moments in time? If you had a journal and had written about those experiences, you could recreate the most wonderful times in your life. You could relive those special times when you were your happiest, and this could bring you more happiness.

Journaling can make you happier and do so much for your life. How do I know? Here is the beginning of my journaling story….

When I was 12 years old my parents left me and my two younger sisters in the back of our old powder-blue station wagon as they went shopping for two hours (yes, they could do that back then). We had to entertain ourselves without fighting, which usually meant do not even look at your sisters! I was the oldest, extroverted, and "in charge." Bossy by nature, I thought I would talk to my sisters, but my middle sister was always very quiet and loved to color. She had three coloring books with her as well as a brand new box of 64 crayons. My youngest sister loved to sleep; she was already snoring quietly. I only had to entertain myself and not get bored and start bothering my sisters with my nonstop talking.

I had purchased a small book with a horse on the cover, assuming it was a book about horses. I had read *Misty of Chincoteague* and all of *The Black Stallion* books. I was ready for a wonderful horse story to keep me occupied and out of trouble. When I opened the book there were no words; the book was blank. It had lines but no words; no story. Imagine my surprise.

I was not sure what to do right away. It took me a while, but I finally realized that it was a journal. I had a pencil in my backpack and started writing in the little book. This was my first introduction to journaling; I have been journaling at least once each month for the past 43 years. For the first twenty years I kept what I call a regular journal, then I expanded to keep other categories of journals.

I would like to share my journal experiences with you because journaling has helped me so many times in my life. My hope is that journaling will help you with whatever is not positive in your life and also to keep a record of the many positives in your life.

Organization of the Journal Book

A friend and coach of mine told me that the organization of this journal book, about journals, is like an episode from the TV sitcom *Seinfeld*, where the crazy character, Kramer, wrote a coffee table book, about…coffee table books. You can use this book to journal and it is a book about journals. The first part of the book discusses aspects of journaling: a history of journaling, who journals, why journaling is helpful, how it can help in life and work, and how to journal. The main part of the book has examples of thirty different kinds of journals. I am sure you can find one that interests you.

Each chapter begins with the title of the journal and a definition/description of the specific journal. Next, I give a real-life example of how I use or have used this journal. Then I will show a picture or some sort of an illustration of the inside of the journal and how I have used it. Next, I'll give examples of how other people have used these journals. Finally, there will be a section where you (the reader) can write what you think about each journal. Feel free to write if you would use the journal yourself or if you could give this journal as a gift to someone. Also, write your feelings about each journal in this book. Do you feel excited about starting, or repulsed that someone would actually journal about this topic? Write examples about what you would write about. Jot down ideas, words, or lists of things that you would put in each specific journal.

There are a few ways to use this book. You can read linearly, from start to finish. You can use this book as a workbook to journal your thoughts as you explore the different categories of journals. You can begin your journey by jumping from journal to journal, reading about the journals that interest you the most. I invite you to make notes in this book at the end of each journal description, decide if this is a journal that you could use or not. If it is a journal that you are interested in trying, then do more research or just jump in! If not, make a note "not for me"— then move on to one that is more interesting to you. I have listed over 30 different styles of journals for your discovery journey. And there may be more categories of journals out there for you to enjoy.

I promise that when you finish reading this book you will be excited to start writing a journal. The only question will be which sort of journal should I start? Now you are on your exhilarating ride to journaling. I wish you the very best experiences on your journey to journal! Have fun.

I define journaling as *writing your original thoughts, ideas, and feelings, in a book, blog or online app at least one time per month for a specific purpose*, as opposed to a "diary," which is an accounting of your day-to-day events. Journaling has become a habit for me. I relax when I write down my thoughts, feelings, and ideas. Throughout all of the years that I have been journaling I have decided to create other journals besides my original format. Journaling has helped me in so many ways since I began that first "horse" journal in 1975. When I think of the word "Journal", it reminds me of the word journey. None of the definitions that I have researched make that connection. *The Oxford English Dictionary* says that the word is of Old French or Latin origin: "Late Middle English (originally denoting a book containing the appointed times of daily prayers): from Old French *jurnal*, from late Latin *diurnalis* (see *diurnal*)." But, for me I think of a journal as a place to record my journey about a particular subject for a specific purpose.

I have many, many journals that I keep in boxes in my storage closets and many on the bookshelf in my office. The picture shows three shelves of my bookshelf in my office. These are completed journals that document my journey through life. I also have a small box of unused journals in a closet in my office. Whenever I am in a store and I see an empty journal book that looks interesting, calming, or purely resonates with me, I buy it and put it in my box. This way when I finish a journal, I can start another one immediately. Usually, during this process I copy the same format and write the title and date on the front page. These journals on my bookshelf are from the past ten years. I keep them if I have a question about my past – I can go back to that book and find the date to see if I wrote about the event. Sometimes, I am faced with

the same dilemma in life and I remember dealing with it before. I ask myself, "What was I thinking when I made those decisions?" I can find out by reading my journal and reliving my journey.

The reason I created this book for you, dear reader, is to introduce you to the world of journaling, to help you discover if journaling is indeed for you, and which journal is best for you. I believe that each of us has unique gifts and talents, and our purpose in life is to share those gifts with other people to help them with their journey. One of my gifts is the ability to journal and to write about many of the different types of journals. My wish is that you read this book with your unique gifts and talents in mind and discover the perfect journal to document your thoughts, ideas, and experiences so that you may share with others to help them learn and grow.

I hope that you enjoy each story in the different categories of journals described. I intentionally used storytelling for the best entertainment, and looked for journal entries that told a story. Feel free to use this book as a starting point to dive deeper into the journal that you desire. I have listed many references and examples to help you start your journey into journaling your way.

After reflecting on my many years of journaling I realized that I have experienced many benefits. Here is a list of benefits you may receive from journaling.

1. **You can sleep at night.** Before I learned how to journal, I had thoughts invade my brain. It was what meditation experts call monkey brain: "What do I need to do tomorrow? What will I make for breakfast? How will I show up in the big meeting on Tuesday? Did I turn off the light in the TV room?" Now, I journal before bed and I write down all of my thoughts, worries, dreams, and strategies. This helps me delete the random thoughts so I can sleep.

2. **You don't worry anymore.** Recently, I realized that I don't ever have to worry. I have always heard the mantra "live in the present," but I recently learned how to apply it to my life. I write what I am worried about in my journal; then I go about my day. I let my journal worry for me and I take action to solve my issues. We worry about the past or the future. In the present we are living the problem so we are not worrying – we are living.

3. **You don't hold a grudge.** Many of my family members and friends that I know hold grudges. Someone made you upset so you just don't talk to them or you talk about them – neither is a good strategy. I write about what made me upset and keep writing about it – I get my emotions out, then I strategize about what to do in that situation. Then I let it go once I have my plan of action.

4. **You can "remember" the past.** Sometimes the past can be blurry. Most of us cannot remember what we ate for lunch yesterday. I have said to myself, "What was I thinking back then when I made that stupid decision?" Yes, I have gone back years in my journal to try not to make the same mistake again. This is indeed an excellent benefit.

5. **You remember great ideas.** I keep a journal beside my bed because I get great ideas in the night. When your body sleeps, your mind is still processing. I have learned how to ask for an answer to a problem that I have *before* I sleep and my mind will process the answer. This happened to me as I was writing my dissertation. I was fixated on the next step in my theory when at 2 a.m. – BOOM – the idea came to me. Fortunately, I had a journal handy and wrote down my idea – I found it in the morning and totally forgot that I was awake at 2 a.m. It was almost as if someone else wrote the answer to my questions – in my handwriting.

6. **You feel better.** According to Dr. Marty Seligman[1] who wrote the book, *Authentic Happiness* and Robert Emmons[2] with his many books on gratitude, being grateful – giving thanks – makes you happier. Keeping a gratitude journal where you would write five things you were thankful for not more than three times a week seems to be a key to being happier. I have been keeping a gratitude journal for the last five years and I am definitely happier after I write in the journal.

7. **You see answers to your prayers.** I keep a prayer journal. I learned how to do this from my roommate in college. She told me to write the date of the prayer, then the prayer, then the date it was answered across the top of the page. I have been doing this for over 30 years and I can see what my prayers were from the past and how they were answered. I am NOT saying that all prayers will be granted (like a genie), but I can see the date that they were answered. If they were answered "no", it is still answered and maybe something better came long instead of what I originally wanted.

8. **You won't stress out.** Have you ever been so upset and there is absolutely no one to talk to about your issue or you don't want to talk to anyone? When I am so upset that I can't even talk to anyone, I write and write and write. I get it all out. At times, I can't even read what I wrote but that does not matter. I got "it" out onto the paper and out of my brain. This is wonderful "therapy" too.

9. **You won't lose friends.** Have you ever been so upset with someone you love that you spoke to them without your filter? There is no way to take back what you say. If you write in a journal when you are upset with a friend, your friend doesn't need to know what you think or write about him or her. I have done this many times. After my emotions are out, then I can think

logically and strategize about what to do and how to better communicate my issue with my friend.

10. **You will lose weight.** Yes, even Weight Watchers know, that if you write down everything you eat, why you ate, and how you felt about it, you will eat less. This strategy has been proven in many university and independent studies, including WEB MD.[3]

11. **You may write better and faster.** They say that practice makes perfect. In his book *Outliers*, Malcom Gladwell[4] says that after 10,000 hours of practice you can be a "master." The more you write, the better you will get at writing. I have noticed that my thoughts come faster and I can type as I think. It is easier for me to sit down to write now than it was when I was in college. Words, thoughts, ideas come to me faster because I have practiced writing my ideas in a book for so many years.

Diary versus journal

Many people ask what the difference is between a diary and a journal. Even as a child I knew the difference. A diary is a daily log — more of a document of daily routine to remember later. When people write in a diary, it is generally every day without fail. A journal is more spontaneous and topical. When people write in a journal, it is when the mood strikes them or they have something to write about at that time. Journals can be about different topics. Diaries don't require any special writing talent. Sometimes they are lists of what was done at different times of the day. Journal writing can require special skills depending on the nature of the journal. A peer-researched journal with articles about psychology or another discipline would be a good example.

When I was a teenaged girl, many of my friends kept diaries. They would write "Dear Diary" and detail how each day was spent. They would write what classes they had, who they met, and what they ate for each meal in chronological order. A diary could actually be used as a work diary that records what was done that day and what needs to be done tomorrow.

There is a difference between a diary and a journal. A journal is more personal than a diary. In a diary you can keep a record of daily experiences and events that happen to you in your life, whereas journals are more personal. Journals may detail the day but also add an emotional response to the activities, people met, and overall feeling. Journals are usually written from a personal point of view, expressing the thoughts, emotions, and reflections of the writer. There are many styles of journals as documented in this book. Journals lead to personal or professional growth through reflection. They can also be used for goal setting and goal getting. Journals can be used for many purposes and reasons.

History of Journals

The earliest person who journaled was said to be Emperor Marcus Aurelius[5] (26 April 121 – 17 March 180 AD). His journal was later created into a book titled Meditations[6]— a journal of his thoughts, his goals, and other abstractions that were meant only for his eyes.

Others believe the first diary[7] began with Samuel Pepys[8] in fifteenth-century England. Pepys wrote in his journal about his personal life (quarrels with his wife) and current events in London (the Great Fire of 1666).

It is my belief that we can argue that journals started with the cave people 65,000 years ago. Jean Clottes[9], a French prehistorian, believes that "in Europe, the main function of cave paintings was to communicate with the spirit world." "We can be sure that in instances like that, they believed in some sort of spiritual force," says (Benjamin) Smith, a rock art scholar at the University of Western Australia. Smith continues, "And they believed that art, and ritual in relation to art, could affect those spiritual forces for their own benefit. They're not just doing it to create pretty pictures. They're doing it because they're communicating with the spirits of the land." So Smith's reasoning is that cave art is not just art, but a way to communicate and possibly to document and draw (because they had no written language) what was happening in their lives. To me that sounds a bit like journaling.

Famous People who Journaled

Many historical people have journaled, as have modern-day celebrities. Journals have been used by philosophers, scientists, artists, inventors, writers, and explorers for the sake of keeping records, history, and a documentation of their ground-breaking findings.

Author of "_The Chronicles of Narnia: The Lion, the Witch and the Wardrobe_", C. S. Lewis[10], wrote two books about journaling and also journaled himself. Lewis continues to be an influential author of children's books, science fiction, and for writing thought-provoking books with metaphorical religious themes. Other authors such as Virginia Woolf, Ray Bradbury, and Henry David Thoreau journaled and were advocates of journaling.

Scientists like Einstein, Charles Darwin, and Marie Curie journaled to document their revolutionary thoughts, ideas, and inventions. Some journals contained pictures drawn to illustrate new discoveries and theories.

Inventors, for example, Thomas Jefferson wrote journals that held illustrations of new inventions, theories, and architecture.

Common people like Anne Frank[11] and Etty Hillesum[12] became famous because of their journals (diaries) during World War II. Soldiers and civilians alike kept diaries or journals during the American Civil War[13].

Artists Frida Kahlo[14] and Leonardo Di Vinci[15] kept journals. These journals were a mixture of illustrations, art, and poems. Frida Kahlo's journals are covered in writing and drawings that only a tortured soul could create. Di Vinci also kept lists of clothing, mundane tasks, and to-do lists in his 5000 pages of journaling.

Modern day celebrities also journal. Oprah Winfrey[16] claims to have started journaling when she was 15 years old. When she was younger she wrote about teen angst issues including boys, being overweight, and what others thought about her. She says she wasted so much time thinking about what others thought. One of the best quotes I've heard is "It is none of my business what you think about me." This phrase is also a title of a book, *What You Think of Me is None of My Business*[17], by Terry Cole-Whittaker. Similar to my journal journey, when Oprah was in her 40s she started a gratitude journal[18], which she has kept for over 10 years. Oprah claims this changed her life. British actress Emma Watson[19] says in an interview[20] that she is an "obsessive diarist and journaler." She notes that she has at least 10 different types of journals, such as dream, yoga, network, an acting journal, and collage books.

America's first self-help book was Benjamin Franklin's *Book of Virtues*[21], based on a working journal he created when he was only 20 years old to document how well (or not) he improved his life. This information was also added to his autobiography. He identified 13 virtues and created a grid to chart a year's progress focusing on one virtue each week and, eventually, covering all 13, four times a year. He mentions at the beginning of the book that as he focused on one virtue, another would be his nemesis. In this journal he lists quotes that inspire him, daily tasks (almost a to-do list), and feelings, thoughts, and conclusions to make his life better. He mentions friends' comments, advice, and how he struggles with these virtues.

Many famous people in all walks of life have journaled. Most of these people I have listed are famous, but for each famous person think of how many others who are not famous but kept journals. Journal writing has been around since man could write (or draw) and it is here to stay. There are so many benefits to journal writing. So many people write only for themselves, others create books out of their journals, and still others only share them with close friends or use them for documentation. It seems that journal writing is easy for a handful of people; however, others are not sure how to even start. I hope that this book helps you to choose the kind of journal you wish to use and helps you begin your own journal journey.

How to Journal

There has been much written about how to journal. Many people say that they are not disciplined enough to journal. To that statement I say "bah!" You do not have to be disciplined to journal. It should be relaxing, peaceful, and enjoyable. Here are a few ideas.

1. Find a journal with which you really resonate – something pretty if that is what you like, something leather or business-like, or something practical. Or if you love to type, try online journaling or blogging. You have to want to physically pick up the journal or go to that site as a habit.

2. Write in your journal when you want to write. Don't pressure yourself with self-imposed rules about when or how often you should write in your journal. Try to write at least once a month to keep your journal going, but it is fine if you put your journal aside for a while and pick it up again. Now, if it is a business journal, I would suggest writing after each meeting. Even if you simply write a sentence or a few phrases, it will prompt your mind about the meeting specifics and how you felt about the meeting.

3. Find a place where you feel comfortable and will not be interrupted — except by your pet. I choose a specific seat on the couch that is on my lanai overlooking a small lake outside. If I need inspiration, I watch birds flying or ducks quacking. Writing in nature always works for me. When it is cold, I move to the couch in my library. I need to be comfortable when I write and always have hot tea or water (or both) near me. Find out what works for you by experimenting with different places to write. You could go to places to write. If you like people around for inspiration, you could go to a library or coffee shop. Writing on the beach or at a park is an option for those who love nature but also want people nearby. Decide if you need silence or a steady buzz of white noise to motivate your writing.

4. Keep your journal in a safe place where you know no one will be tempted to read it. I have had a couple of journals with a locks on them. I would put the key in my jewelry box. But, most of the journals

have locks that are not that sturdy. You could lock the journal in your safe or in a locked drawer. I have been lucky and have never lived with anyone who thought my journals were valuable. I have storage boxes full of journals in a closet under my staircase at home and a bookshelf full of journals with only one shelf full of empty journals.

5. Choose a certain time to journal. Many people love to get up early in the morning, drink their coffee, and sit with their thoughts. I personally love to write on the weekends or after breakfast (especially on the weekends). Some of you are night owls and like to write before you go to sleep at night. You don't always have to write at these times, but finding a time when you like to journal may help make it a habit.

Once you are settled...you may ask yourself, "What do I write?" Here are specific ways to get started.

1. Listen to yourself. Everyone has that self-talk in his or her head. If it is old tapes from your childhood, music, or the nagging of all of the things you have to do or what you should have done, I would suggest listening to your inner self and start writing. Who cares what is on the paper? These words are only for you and no one else.

2. Be compassionate. Write with no judgement. Don't worry about anything at all — just write. Don't worry about punctuation, grammar, or spelling. Remember: no one will be reading your journal and you can be compassionate with yourself if you do make some mistakes.

3. Decide what interests you and write about it. Write about your passions, your day, your friends or family.

4. Get your journal and set it out where you can see it each day. I keep journals right on my kitchen bar so I can grab them when I go outside to sit on my lanai. I keep another on the table by my bed. Now that I think about it, I should keep one in the bathroom! If your journal is out where you can see it, it will be easier to reach. If you have a rough day or a most wonderful day you can write about it.

5. When you have a bit of quiet time, sit with your journal and write about what you see around you. Simply, starting is helpful.

6. Sometimes looking at a blank book is intimidating. When I get a new journal I have a format of how it should go. This is my method for my "normal" journal. I start by writing my name and phone number on the front pages. Next I write the date that I started the journal with a squiggle underneath for the date when I end. Then I write my goals on one of the front

pages. I usually copy the goals from my old journal, but if you are just starting you can write a few goals here. Then I go to the back of the journal and make a table for my prayer journal.

7. Plan the day in your calendar ahead of time and schedule your first journaling sessions. Decide that you will journal for only five minutes. Set a timer for only five minutes. If you decide to keep going – GREAT! If not, try this again. Maybe you are a five minute journaler.

American author Natalie Goldberg[22] says, "If you feel bored or uncomfortable as you're writing, ask yourself what is bothering you and write about that. Sometimes your creative energy is like water in a kinked hose, and before thoughts can flow on the topic at hand, you have to straighten the hose by attending to whatever is preoccupying you."

Prolific author Lisa Shea[23] has written 11 books on journaling and journaling prompts. There are also many other books that offer journaling prompts. If you are unsure what to write and cannot put your feelings into words, these authors can help you focus on your self and narrow down your topic so you can write. Personally, I have never used journal prompts because I only write when I have something to write about, and I now have a habit of writing. Journal prompts are wonderful to help you create that habit of writing.

TYPES OF JOURNALS

This next section of the book will focus on the many different categories of journals that seemed interesting to me. This is not a finite list of journals. I wanted to give you, my reader, a starting point to decide for yourself which kind of journal is best for you. If you have journaled in the past or read about journals, you can compare your experiences to mine and to the examples in this book. If you are new to journaling, please read about all of the different styles of journals. Use the space provided at the end of each section to journal along in this book, discovering what works for you and what will not work for you. This book is meant to be a journey to discover the best sort of journal for you now, at this time, in this place.

REGULAR JOURNAL

A regular journal is one which you would write your thoughts, ideas, feelings, or whatever interests you at that moment. Each entry is dated, but you don't have to feel the pressure of writing in this journal each day. Write in a regular journal when you want to get your thoughts out of your head, document something that happened, write something emotional that you can't talk to anyone about yet. There are many reasons to write. Find your reasons and write when the mood strikes you. I would suggest if you start to feel pressure to write in the journal, then take a break — journals should not cause stress.

I started a generic journal when I was 12 years old and would write pretty frequently, but then I'd take weeks before I wrote again. Soon, writing in a journal became a habit; then it became a life saver. I wrote mostly about school and my friends and family while I was in grade school. I wrote mostly about school, swim team, and my boyfriend in high school. In college I wrote about the drama of breaking up with my boyfriend, my friends, and more boyfriend drama. I also started writing other kinds of journals in college; however, I had no idea that they were called journals at the time. I started a spiritual journal on my own and a dream journal as a class assignment. After grad school in my 20s, I wrote about my job, boyfriend, wonderful new friends, and my new "home" in Maryland. In my 30s I wrote more about my job and my husband and my new family in Texas. I wrote about starting a new business and the places I visited. I wrote about my marriage. In my 40s I wrote about my accomplishments, my failures, and my newfound independence as a single mom. I wrote about dating, my job, and my amazing child. I also started writing different styles of journals when I was around 35 years old. I branched into gratitude, goals, and a night journal. In my 50s I continued to keep four journals going and write in them often. I also write in others less frequently.

I never thought of myself as a writer, even when I researched and wrote a dissertation that was published two weeks before my fortieth birthday. I always said that I don't really like to write. Actually, I love to write down my thoughts; I love to research. I just don't like the editing part or the detailed proof reading. I hired my dear friend Sandy Beherend as my editor for my dissertation, and now I have another dear friend and colleague edit this book. It seems that I really do like to write, not edit, so journaling is perfect for me. I write stream of consciousness, which is fine because no one reads my journal except me.

After the first day I did not write in my horse journal for about three weeks; then I started writing five times a week, then I took a month break. I can't remember the thoughts of my 12-year-old self, but it is comical to read what I wrote so long ago. I seldom went back to my 20-year-old journals until I made my last move. I scanned some of them while I moved the journals from an old cardboard box to a new plastic bin. Most my old journals are in a storage space in my new house. I have the last 10 years of journals on a bookshelf in my office to read if I have questions.

Recently, I was asked to testify in a personal injury trial because I witnessed an event and the lawyer wanted me to remember it from two years ago. That event is plain as day in my mind because I had never witnessed something like that before or after. I walked into the rest room during a conference and a woman was on the floor. She had slipped on water and showed me her kneecap which was split in two. I went back to my journals to see what I had written about that day. I realized I had not written anything that day. I was in the process of selling my house in Virginia and buying a house in Florida. I was consumed with that train of thought and did not even bother to write about the event that day. So, be aware that not all of the events in your journey will be documented in your journal. But, I now have learned that if anything out of the ordinary happens, definitely, write about it. I find journaling to be a huge learning opportunity too.

Are you interested in writing your thoughts, ideas and feelings in a journal? Would you feel comfortable writing when you are in the mood? Do you feel better after you get your thoughts and emotions out of your head?

I would use a regular journal   I would not use a regular journal

Notes:

JOURNAL TO RELAX

So many times I feel my body tighten up and feelings of anxiety and stress come over me. I realize that my breathing is shallow and I feel tense. I have learned to notice this feeling and instead of eating or feeling grumpy, I decide to journal. Once I get my journals and sit in a quiet spot, I begin to relax. As soon as I start to write about anything, my breathing returns to a slower pace. It does not matter what I write about, I feel all of the negative energy and stress disappear. Journal writing relaxes me and makes me grateful that I have a moment to sit quietly and write.

When people meet me they realize that I am a huge extrovert. I love to talk to people. I love to get to know other people to hear their stories, and share mine too. No one is a stranger to me. I talk to people at the grocery store, at gas stations, and yes, even in elevators. Many times I have people ask me, "Do you really need that quiet time? You seem to like to be with people more than like your time alone." I love both. I enjoy being with people and I like my quiet time. The journal writing helps me be grateful when I write about my experiences with my friends and family, or work.

The process of sitting quietly and concentrating on one thing, writing in my journal, reminds me of mindfulness practices. Instead of focusing on my breathing, I focus on what I am writing. I let the thoughts flow and write them down. Once I write down my thoughts, I let them go. This relaxes me and gets rid of my "monkey mind.[1]" This journaling practice is very similar to the practice of meditation. I have been told that to meditate I need to sit quietly, close my eyes, and focus on my breathing. If thoughts come into my head, and they will, I gently push them away, like shooing a little puppy out of the room.

Sometimes, I relive my wonderful experiences. This experience is called savoring. Fred Bryant and Joseph Veroff have a book called *Savoring: A New Model of Positive Experience*. Savoring enhances the actual experience. For example, I look forward to my vacation. I imagine where I will go and what I will do. Then, while on vacation I live in the moment and have amazing adventures. After the vacation I savor the memories. I relive the experiences and that may be even better than the actual experience. Do you need to relax? Has stress taken over your life? Would writing in a journal relax you?

I would use a journal to relax   I would not use a regular journal to relax

Notes:

PRAYER JOURNAL

A prayer journal is a place to write down your prayers. Document the things that you wish for in life: things that you want for yourself or other people.

My college roommate went to Bible study groups and taught me how to keep a prayer journal. I put this section in the back of my standard, everyday journal and do not have a separate journal for my prayers. The journal is organized very simply. At the top of each page I write "Date," "God Hear my Prayer," and "Date Answered." Then I draw lines between these words from the top to the bottom of the page. It looks like a table.

Date	Hear My Prayer	Date Answered
2-2-17	Please God let me get an A on the history test tomorrow.	YES 2-5-17
2-4-17	Help Carol get well soon – before she has to give the speech next week.	

Next, I put the date that I first thought about the prayer. Then I write my prayer as descriptively as I can write it. I put the names of people and the description in this section. Sometimes it is a short prayer; other times I can get quite detailed in my request. Finally, I write the date that the prayer is answered and the answer. If the prayer is not answered in the time I have the journal. When this happens I either transfer the prayer to the new journal or stop praying that prayer.

Groups have prayer journals. Catholic churches say "Lord hear our prayer" as someone reads a list from a prayer journal. There are prayer groups[1] that have journals. A person from the group writes down a name and a prayer in the journal. Next, the entire group prays for the person or a family. These journals are wonderful for follow up because it helps with one's faith in God or good: the faith that our prayers will be answered. *Proof* that our prayers were answered.

Do you pray? Would you like to keep a record of all of the prayers that are answered? Is a prayer journal for you?

I would use a prayer journal   I would not use a prayer journal

Notes:

DREAM JOURNAL

A dream journal is a book where you write down your dreams as soon as you wake up. When I was in college in 1983 I took a psychology class where we were told to keep a journal of our dreams. We were directed to keep an empty book (notebook, blank sketch book, or composition book) near our bed and, when we woke from a dream, to write down the dream.

I did this for ten weeks and had a number of very strange experiences. When I first started I would wake up in the middle of the night and turn the light on and write what I could remember of my dream. If I did not wake up, I would try to remember my dreams in the morning. I was lucky that I had my own dorm room (I was a resident assistant) at that time.

At first, I could not remember each dream or all of the details. After about two weeks, I remembered all of my dream details. When the quarter ended and I did not have to do this assignment anymore, I could not stop the remembering. Many dreams I did not wish to remember, but I could not stop. For some reason this practice stayed with me for a while. Finally, after about three months I stopped remembering every single dream and detail. I don't think it is wise to remember each dream. I guess that a few dreams must be there to flush out the bad stuff.

You can also get a book of dreams to find out more about different types of dreams or symbolism. For example, *The Dream Dictionary from A – Z*[1] is a book that notes many different type of dreams and symbolism for things that happen or objects in a dream. Symbols are organized alphabetically to more easily research what each means. For example, I often dream that I am flying. This book suggests that flying in a dream can represent high hopes or feeling great about career or goals. Freud[2] has his own version of what flying represents in dreams if you are interested.

What a dream journal looks like

Date	Dream	People	Feelings	Ideas
3-04-17	I was flying around the clouds, then lightly landed in a garden of roses. I had the feeling of bliss.	only me.	Flying freely Bliss Happiness	Flying means I am happy about my goals. Roses symbolize love and faithfulness. Maybe I am happy in my relationship?
3-17-17	Another flying dream. I was flying over a large body of water, maybe it was a bay because there were battleships and oil drums. Maybe a harbor. I was actually in a place with many oil drums. It was dark and I was trying to save someone. I was looking for something.	Me but I was looking for some one.	I was trying to solve a problem. A mystery maybe.	I was trying to help someone. Do I have an unsolved problem in my life now? Who am I looking for?

Are you interested in your dreams? Would you like to remember your dreams when you wake up in the morning? Do your dreams tell you something?

I would use a dream journal   I would not use a dream journal

Notes:

NIGHT JOURNAL

A night journal is physically located near your bed. It is used so that when you wake up in the middle of the night with a "great" thought you can write it down and not forget it in the morning. You can also use this journal to help problem-solve while you sleep. I had heard that the mind is like a computer. My ex-husband, a computer genius, used to call it back-burner processing. My mind would get a thought, then think about it while I was asleep – then the great thought would appear (as if by magic). Then, I would wake up and write it in my night journal. This can be a conscious processing or randomly, waking up in the middle of the night with no plan for problem solving.

When I was working on my Ph.D. dissertation I kept a notebook by my bed to help me capture thoughts that I might forget. I would write my dissertation from 8:30 a.m. – 6:00 p.m. each day and try to put the pieces together. I asked myself, "How do all of these things fit together?" Then, one night I woke up with the answer to my question. It amazingly happened late one night – so I wrote the answer in my notebook, which happened to be next to my bed. The next morning, I realized that I had the answer that had been evading me for the last two months! The answer to the question that my advisor had been asking me for a while. My main discovery in the dissertation all came together and I could tie all of the various pieces together with a conclusion or at least a theory.

This was amazing to me. Now, when I have a difficult problem, I think about the issue before I fall asleep. Many times I wake up with the answer.

Yes, I am an Elvis fan and this is a paper journal with a picture of young Elvis on every page. (Thank you very much.) As you can see, when I wake up in the middle of the night and write, it is not neat at all. I write all over the paper. I don't even use the lines. The idea is to get all of my thoughts out of my head and onto the paper so I can read it in the morning. I use a lot of bullets because many times when I wake up after a dream or idea, I cannot write a paragraph or even a complete sentence.

Do what is best for you. Some people have a recorder or their phone handy. They wake up and speak while recording their thoughts. I find

What a night journal looks like:

that I cannot do this because I do not want to wake my husband next to me. I go into the bathroom, turn on the light, and write my thoughts while he sleeps peacefully. Other people find that talking and recording works better for them.

Another definition of a night journal would be to journal at night before you go to sleep. Journaling before sleep is a great idea for those of us who have so many thoughts wandering around in our brains. I've heard it called "monkey mind" because the thoughts are as crazy as a monkey swinging around playing. Linda Wasmer Andrews in her article "Journaling Before Bed Can Help Ward Off Sleeplessness"[1] states that if you write about positive events you will sleep better. Also, if you make this part of your nighttime routine, you will train your brain, so that when you write and get all of your thoughts on paper they will stay there and not play around in your mind at night. I would not call this a "night journal". You can use *any* type of journal, but write at night to get these benefits.

Do you wake up in the middle of the night with thoughts, but then forget them by morning? Would you like to remember your dreams? Do you need to get all of your feelings and emotions written down before you sleep?

I would use a night journal   I would not use a night journal

Notes:

POSSIBILITIES/INTENTIONS JOURNAL

After watching the movie, *The Last Holiday*[1] with Queen Latifah and LL Cool J, I was taken with the idea of a "book of possibilities." Queen Latifah's character created this form of journal/book, which showed pictures of what she wanted in her life: all of the things on her bucket list. I would compare her book in the movie to a scrapbook. It showed pictures and had a story on the same page. A book version of a vision board if you will. I created my very own book of possibilities. I have a special journal where I write what I want to happen in the future. I write lists of things that I wish to happen in my life. I enjoy writing, so I write stories about my future. I would date the page then write my "story." Setting intentions or writing "your story" is easier than you may believe. All you need to do is come up with a positive intention or a story to describe and sum up your future you.

For example, in January of 2016, I was living in Springfield, Virginia, dreaming of selling my house, leaving my job, and moving to sunny Florida. I loved the house that I had lived in for 19 years because I renovated the entire house with a new kitchen, all new bathrooms, and a most magnificent addition. It had a huge closet, bathroom and yoga room. Finally, it was my dream house. I hoped that I could find a house that I loved just as much, only in Florida. So, I wrote the date 1-17-16 in my special journal and wrote about my "new" house. I described that it was 15 minutes from my favorite beach (Anna Maria Island), it had a pool and hot tub with a "waterfall" within a cage on the lanai to keep out the bugs. I wrote that I would be looking at water from my bedroom and from the pool area. I described the kitchen as being as big as the one I had in Virginia, the bathroom with a separate toilet stall, a walk-in closet, and a soaking tub. I also imagined the neighborhood had great neighbors. In Virginia, I had wonderful neighbors for years, but the old folks like me were moving out and new neighbors with young children were moving into the neighborhood. I wrote about how helpful my new neighbors would be and how I could still have my annual neighborhood holiday party.

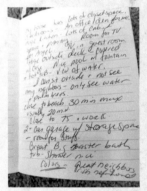

In January of 2017, I was writing in this same journal about my wonderful new client and how much I loved to help her with my business when I decided to read one of the past stories. It was about my house. I actually got everything correct except for the soaking tub. I am now living in the house that I wrote about 6 months before I moved. I read a similar story about a vision board in the book *The Secret* by Rhonda Byrne[2].

Here are several ideas about how to start your possibilities/intention journal:

Write the date that you wrote the intention. Then write the date that it happened. I put the date I first wrote the intention in the upper right corner. When it came true, I write a note on the bottom with the date I realized it came to into being my present reality.

Take your intention/possibility seriously. Believe it. When I write my story about what I want to happen in the future I try to make it the best story possible. I make sure that I have real places and real people even if I have never been to these places or met these people yet. I make sure I am very detailed with my writing and my story. If you are having difficulty believing, use words like "I choose to be…," "I am so happy that…," "I expect that…."

Write about what you want. What you really, really want. (Thanks, Spice Girls). You don't have to limit yourself to what you have now. Write about ANYTHING, any things, feelings, experiences, or relationships. ANYTHING you wish to have come true. I always go above and beyond what I think is possible. It is your story so make it your BEST future. Write as yourself! You only need these intentions for YOU! Use your own words and slang. Be your unique and authentic you. Write with passion and feeling. Be accepting of yourself and your beliefs. Do not judge yourself, your statements, or your new reality. Don't let your version of "reality" stop you. Go for the moon!

Write about the new opportunity as if you are already there. Do NOT worry or write about HOW you are going to get there. Speak in the first person. Use "I" and "me" statements. Use the most powerful words ever: "I am." Write in present tense. Close your eyes and imagine that you are already experiencing the wonderful things that you desire. "This is happening now." I would write that "I am living in a house 15 minutes from the Moose Lodge on Anna Maria Island." Don't say, "I will" or "It could be" – be positive be in the NOW. For example, I would write, "I have a loving, kind, and generous husband." Special note: As I was doing the final editing of this book, I realized that when I wrote the last sentence I was not married. I am now married to a "loving, kind, and generous husband." This stuff works!

Write with gratitude statements from the heart. Write as an expression of "grateful having," rather than wanting or needing. A number of examples are listed here: "I am so grateful and happy that I have a best friend who loves me and cares about my well being," or "Thank you that I now have my perfect job." Write about the things you have and are grateful for now. Give yourself kudos for the strengths and skills that you already have too! You can mix up what you already have with what you wish you had.

Write in the positive. Instead of "I will not eat sugar" write, "I will eat healthy foods." Use "I am" or "I do." Do NOT use the word NOT. If you tell a child not to go into a room, he is more curious and of course will go into the room. When I was a lifeguard we were taught to say, "walk" instead of "Don't run around the pool deck."

Write in your learning mode. If you are more visual, use imagery (word pictures). If auditory, use sounds (*crunch!*). If kinesthetic, use emotions, feelings, or movement (actions).

It is important that you only write affirmations for yourself – you cannot change other people. For example, if you wish that your husband would stop watching football and do laundry on the weekend – write from your point of view. You cannot change your husband. You can only change yourself. Sure, if that is your dream, go ahead and write about the one weekend during football season that you and he cleaned the entire house together. Write in first person and detail your feelings and emotions.

Have FUN! If writing the details is not fun – don't write the details! Write what feels best for YOU. It is about you.

Change, upgrade, and evolve as the intentions manifest themselves. Now that I have my "dream" home in Florida, I decided to upgrade my possibilities. I would like a home on the bay. At the present time I cannot afford the homes that I have been perusing using the online real estate applications, but I can always write about that beautiful 1.2 million-dollar home with the view of the bay. Sure, I am very happy with my new home, but why not dream?

This style of journal gives me hope that I can live a better life, that good things will happen – even if it simply a story I tell myself. I find that I am much more positive after writing in my "possibilities journal." I also love to go back to that journal and see what has changed – my dreams coming true.

Do you want your dreams to come true? Do you believe in affirmations and write them down randomly? Would you like a place to write all of your intentions and see them come true?

I would use a possibilities/intentions journal   I would not use a possibilities/intentions journal

Notes:

BUSINESS – WORK JOURNAL

While researching a definition of business journal I found results suggesting financial journals. Most businesses keep financial journals. The business journal that I am describing is not a financial journal; rather, it is more of a diary of what happens day to day, at meetings and reactions of how you and others acted or reacted emotionally during the workday. Some might say that this is called "note taking" and many meetings have "secretaries" to keep the minutes. An article by William Arruda in *Forbes* magazine[1] states that "keeping a job journal is the one thing successful people do every day." Personal business journals also record emotions and any other actions or reactions during a meeting. These journals are the individual's perspectives and perceptions of what happened during the meetings. It is important to note that each individual has a different perception of what happened during each meeting. But, by documenting your own thoughts and ideas, you can better reflect, brainstorm, and make decisions.

Dan Ciampa wrote a wonderful article in the *Harvard Business Review*, "The More Senior Your Job Title, the More You Need to Keep a Journal[2]." I could not agree more. He states that he "kept a journal through 12 years as chairman and CEO and have since recommended it to people moving into any senior position for the first time." He suggests that we write the journal in a book and not use a digital device to slow down the process, causing reflection and so that "learning is maximized." He acknowledges that journaling takes time and, as we know in business time is money, but Ciampa believes that the reflection process and "slowing things down leads to better-thought-through, more effective judgement and to learning what to do more of and what to change." His conclusion is that all leaders should include a personal journal in their "toolkit."

In the article mentioned above, Mr. Ciampa describes the way he creates each entry.

1. Note the essential reason for that outcome – root cause analysis (use the 5 why method: ask "why" five times)

2. Recall emotions that affected decisions and describe in great detail

3. Identify what you can learn and do differently next time (best practices)

Using this method, you can document the meeting, reflect, and analyze the results. You will have summarized the important parts of the meeting, analyzed the outcomes, reflected on emotions and created best practices for your next meeting.

Skip Prichard, a businessman turned blogger and self-proclaimed Twitter addict, wrote a very good blog about "Why Journaling Makes Better Leaders[3]," in which he states that journaling made him a better leader. He shares his expertise and experience that journaling…

- makes you more organized, especially if you write each morning and determine your priorities for the day.

- improves decision making (which is critical for leaders), helping you prepare for meetings and work the issue by generating alternatives, other perspectives, and new ideas.

- improves demeanor, attitude and judgment by writing to become more self-aware of your attitude. It gives you a place to vent your emotions, clarify your motivations, and connect with your energy.

- helps you focus on your intentions.

Albert Bandura, a cognitive psychologist, defines self-efficacy[4] as "an individual's belief in his or her capacity to execute behaviors necessary to produce specific performance attainments (Bandura, 1977, 1986, 1997)." I think of it as self-fulfilling prophecy. If you think you can succeed, you will. If you think you can't succeed, you can't. It is important for leaders to focus intentions and believe they will succeed. Finally, journaling helps create positive reinforcement. Having a place to see all of the positive successes in your business and life helps us all to be more positive. Most people I know would rather have a positive boss than a negative boss.

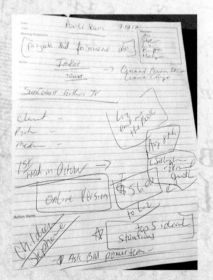

I always kept amazing notes for myself for every meeting I attended, even if it was solely between me and one other person. Other people that were at the meeting would ask me questions later and I would say, "Let me get my notes." They knew that I could describe almost word for word what was actually said during meetings. One of my supervisors realized I did this and told me, "Don't write this down." "*Hmmmm*", I contemplated. I still have journals filled with notes from meetings from my last job stored away. I keep them just in case I need to refer back to them about something that I may have forgotten. They are stored in chronological order. I would always include the date, meeting topic, who was at the meeting and why I thought the meeting was taking place (objectives). If there was an agenda, I would staple it to the notebook at the beginning of the entry. I have very messy writing and tend to write in drawings, so I learned how to create mind map[5] for meetings. It is much more efficient. This way, instead of going back and squishing in notes (if a speaker added information to something that he or she was talking about earlier), I would merely draw another branch. This way all of the like information would be together and make more sense.

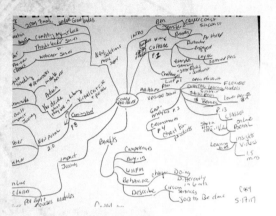

To create a mind map, use the paper in a landscape page orientation (more width than height). Put the center idea in a circle in the middle. Start at one o'clock and draw a line up and over to the right. Always try to put your words parallel to each other so you can read them later. Write the first main idea, then use lines as branches off of this main thought. Write short phrases or one or two words to summarize this thought. For example, when the speaker in the meeting moves to the next topic (or person), draw another branch at two o' clock or three o'clock (whenever you have room). Draw branches off of this main topic and continue around the circle. If the meeting is longer than your mind map, start another one. The idea is to have summaries of the main topic in fewer words (key words) and a record of what happened at the meeting. There is also software available to create a mind map online if this is easier than drawing in a journal.

So, are you a leader at work? Would you like to be more organized, efficient, and positive? Are you interested in using a mind map or other tool to take notes and journal?

I would use a business journal   I would not use a business journal

Notes:

NETWORKING JOURNAL

A networking journal will detail each of your contacts and list all of the information about that contact, including meeting notes. A networking journal could be organized by date or alphabetically by the person's last name. An address book with a calendar attached is a good example of a networking journal. The contacts are listed and hyperlinked to dates on the calendar when meetings took place.

The contact information is listed with all information that may be important. Of course, include names and addresses and contact information but, more information should be listed, for example

- Dates and how you met this contact
- Other contacts associated with this contact
- Important dates for the contact
    - Birthdays (theirs, spouse, kids)
    - Anniversaries
    - Work anniversaries
    - Pets

Networking journals can be online contact management systems[1] (CRM). There are many applications to use online in order to manage your contacts, business associates, or leads. Many sales professionals and small business professionals use these tools. These tools are not journals. They are applications used to manage contacts. However, these tools have many uses, for example linking contacts to your email or to an online application (or both).

The calendar section of the journal will list the date and time you met with the person on the calendar. Then that entry can be hyperlinked to a document section. This section will note the important aspects of the meeting: the goal of the meeting, the agenda, takeaways, action plans, or to-do information.

I used to network the WRONG way. I would go to events and get a ton of business cards. When I got back to my office, I would not remember why I had a person's card. Then, I changed my networking strategy. As soon as someone gave me his or her card, I would write notes on the back of the card. That way, when I got back to my office I could follow up more efficiently. But, I still had a ton of cards and did not wish to keep an old-fashioned Rolodex. I then started typing my contacts into Outlook. Now, I use an app to scan the cards and keep them in the app.

When I first began my networking journal, I used a paper journal. I wrote about the contacts as soon as I met them. It was a first impressions journal, at first; then I would leave blank pages to complete after more meetings with that person. Sometimes, I would never meet this person again and these pages would stay blank. This journal eventually stopped working for me because it was not organized very well. I now prefer to have my contacts on an online application. I use Microsoft Outlook for my email and create contacts and write notes about each person.

I also use LinkedIn and Facebook for networking and contacts. These are not journals but social media applications that can achieve the same goal as a networking journal, depending on your goal. I keep my professional contacts on LinkedIn and my personal contacts on Facebook.

Do you have professional or personal contacts that you would like to organize? Would you like to keep better notes as you network?

I would use a networking journal   I would not use a networking journal

Notes:

GRATITUDE JOURNAL

One of my favorite times of the week is when I write in my gratitude journal. A gratitude journal is a place to write all of the things that you are grateful for at that moment. This is a very positive journal and has been shown to generate happiness and positive feelings. According to Robert Emmons[1], Thanks author and leading scientific expert, gratitude has two key components: gratitude is an affirmation of goodness and the sources of this goodness are outside of ourselves. Robert Emmons writes that being grateful – giving thanks – makes you happier. Keeping a gratitude journal where you would write five things you were thankful for not more than three times a week seems to be a key to being happier.

I have been keeping a gratitude journal for the last ten years and I am definitely happier after I write in the journal. When I started the gratitude journal, I wrote ten things for which I was grateful in the journal every day. Sure, I missed a few days, but I did this each time I wrote in my general journal. I kept both journals next to each other on my bedside table because I used to write just before bedtime. Sometimes it was difficult to think of ten things each day, but I thought that was part of the process – it had to be challenging. I have been grateful for my relationships with my family, best friends, and new friends. I have been grateful for the time I had to write in my journal and the peaceful place where I am sitting. There is no right or wrong about being grateful. You can share your gratitude for things of the present or the past that have led to the present. Writing in this journal is all about the moment and feeling grateful in the moment. There are no rules when it comes to writing in this journal. You can do what ever feels like you are sharing your gratitude with yourself and the world.

After reading Emmons' books *Thanks*[2] and *Gratitude Works*[3], I learned that journaling my gratitude should not be challenging. So, I followed his directions the very next day in my gratitude journal, documenting the change and why I was changing my gratitude practice and process. He suggests writing five gratitude entries (at the most) and being more detailed so that I could savor each one with more zest. Also, not to write every day. I suppose there is such a thing as "gratitude burnout." So, instead of writing my ten one-line reasons of why I am grateful, I now write five things and try to give more than one line so I can appreciate the things for which I am grateful. It has been suggested that you write about the things that you have, and also about the things that you don't have. For example, thank you for today's perfect weather. There are places on this earth where people are experiencing flooding and hurricane winds. Be grateful for big things such as your health and little things such as the fresh air you are breathing at that moment. The idea is to feel true gratitude and immerse yourself in the feeling of happiness and joy.

The first picture of the journal is my first page. I like to have a theme or introduction to my gratitude journal and give myself positive words before I start to write each time. Also, notice the heart in the journal. I feel with my heart when I feel gratitude. Gratitude is an emotion that is heartfelt. Sometimes when I am reading after I write in my journal I put my hand over my heart without even thinking that I have moved my hand. For some reason, I think this gesture adds more emotion, more thoughtfulness, and more love to the gratitude thought that I had previously written. The second

image shows a page in my gratitude journal; I tried to find one page where all five entries were on one page. Sometimes I need to have two pages because I try to write more

than two sentences about each thing that I am grateful for that day. And YES, I do have very messy handwriting. That is OK. It is what I choose. Computer savvy people may choose to write their gratitude journal in a Word document or in a blog or on their Facebook page. It does not matter where you write your entries, as long as they are in the same place so you can go back and read them when you are feeling dissatisfied with your life and you need a reminder of why you are grateful.

Are you grateful for your life? Do you need more happiness and positivity in your life? Do you want to have better health and energy in your day? Would a gratitude journal work for you?

I would use a gratitude journal   I would not use a gratitude journal

Notes:

MONEY EVIDENCE JOURNAL

Do you wish you had more money? The idea of this journal is to get more money and being grateful for what you have so you will get more. Specifically, you would write the date and details each time you get money, win something, or save money. This journal is based on the idea of manifesting: the more you think about something, the more it is likely to happen. So, the more I think about getting money, and the more I write about getting money, the more it will happen.

Many times I win something or get unexpected checks or save money and then I forget. I know that I win things often. In fact, I have been told that I win things more than most people. This has been the case since I was young. I won random raffles and games of chance. When there were fishbowls in restaurants I would put in my business card and days or weeks later I would get a call that I had won.

A few examples are:

- Lunch for 8 people at Noodles and Company to taste the new menu
- 12 burritos at Chipotle
- Free drinks at Starbucks
- Lunch for 4 at Potbelly

Sometimes, I do not even get a ticket for a raffle because I want to let someone else win. I win door prizes, drawings, raffles, and contests often. I tell people that I am lucky because that is how it seems to me. Most people I know do not win things as often as I do. One of the reasons that I started this journal was to prove to myself that I do win more than most people. I wanted to see exactly how often I win things: is it once a month, once every two months, or once every six months?

But, this journal is not all about what you have won in a raffle, lottery, or contest. I also note any variety of financial gain or savings. I also note anytime I thought I was going to spend money and I did not have to spend any. These reasons may include cancellation of the event where I would normally have to pay, postponing payment, or a free meal. I also count coupons, refunds, and rebates.

In the journal pictures I show the first introduction page and a random page of the journal. The first picture shows my introduction to my money evidence journal. I call it Evidence Journal for Money. I list many affirmations and use dollar signs — $$ — as bullet points.

Many of my affirmations listed are:

$ I win things all of the time

$ I save money

$ I get checks in the mail

$ Money shows up in my bank account

$ People love to pay me

$ I have free-flowing wealth

$ A blissful state of free-flowing wealth

$ Money attraction vibration

$ People invite me to dinner or lunch

Other examples of entries could be:

$ I got paid $2000

$ Joe bought me a cup of tea today

$ I was too busy to go shopping today, thus did not spend any money

$ A $25 check came in the mail

$ I won $4 in Lotto (OK – I spent $10 for that ticket – but this still counts in my book)

$ I won a door prize of a basket with a book and 2 bottles of wine (read between the wines)

$ I won a $50 gift certificate for entering a contest

Later, I re-read my entries in this journal to see how truly fortunate I am in life. I analyze the journal for trends and try to figure out if there is a method or pattern. A recent trend that I noticed is that at least once a month someone gives or buys me something. I have always been very social and generous. Maybe I bought that person something and he or she is returning the favor. Maybe I need to keep track of what I spend as well. For example, I won $4 in the lottery but I spent $10 on the ticket.

The next picture shows a typical page of journal entries. Notice that I always start with the date, then a dash, then the entry. Other entries include

6/19 – Allison cancelled lunch, so I did not spend money. I saved $20

6/20 – Meeting cancelled, $20 refund – credit to be used for the next meeting

7/1 – Got paid Friday $2000

7/2 – Dinner at Mom and Dad's house – Free meal! (priceless)

7/7 – Margaret paid for lunch $75

7/11 – Class was free when I expected to pay $39

I have been keeping this journal now for over a year and I decided to note what I saved or got every day. Sometimes it is as simple as being offered a bottle of water (at the airport that could be worth $2.50) or something happened so I did not spend money. I am amazed that I do get something or save every day. Every once in a while I can't think of anything, so once I had a meeting cancelled so I wrote "free time." That is a new way to think about free. I was thinking about adding up all of the money I received over the year but a few of the entries are priceless, like dinner at my parents' house or free time. Most times, I find that this journal makes me realize how wealthy and lucky I am, and that makes me happy.

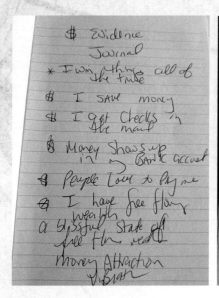
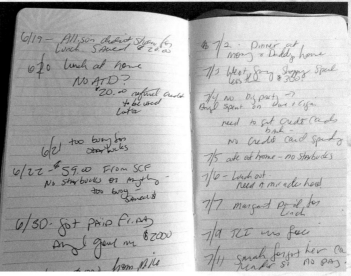

Do you need more money in your life? Do you need to save money? Would you like to win more or get free things in the mail? Do you wish to feel happier? Would you use a money evidence journal?

I would use a money evidence journal   I would not use a money evidence journal

Notes:

TRAVEL JOURNAL

A travel journal is a book or online journal used to write about your travels, trips, or adventures. It can be organized by date, by country, by state, or by whom you visit. Journalers may like to keep a large journal and document all of their trips in one book. Others like to keep a different journal for each trip. Travel journals may contain photos or contain only text. Some contain drawings, maps, or other illustrations.

When I traveled to Peru for two weeks, I kept a special journal solely for this trip. I wrote in the journal each day, and possibly twice a day because my experiences were so different from what I was used to at home. I wrote about where we were going and where we had been. I wrote detailed stories, including exactly what a person had said. I wrote about my adventures in the rain forest, the people I met, and my reflections. After the group of eight of us would go into the rain forest (jungle) we would return to the boat hot and sweaty. We would take a cold shower (because there was no hot water) and most people would go to the bar at the top of the boat. I would retire to the front of the boat to a little alcove in front of where the captain would be steering. There were three plastic chairs in that little alcove and I would take one and at times the captain would already be sitting in one reading his newspaper. I would take one chair and look over the Amazon River watching the birds fly by. I would feel the warm sunshine on my face and write my thoughts about my adventures. Sometimes, the rocking of the boat, the warmth of the weather, and the quiet would put me to sleep. Yes, the captain would sometimes be asleep as well. I guess he had a reliable first mate.

I also wrote in a travel journal when I went to Cuba. The weather was rainy and windy so we did not get to the beach on that trip. We were on a cruise ship that was anchored in Cienfuegos, so we had a lot of time on the docked ship. We took bus excursions to Havana and Trinidad, Cuba, and saw a lot of the countryside as well as the cities. After our 12-hour excursions I would get back to the cruise ship, take a shower, eat, then write in my travel journal. I enjoy reading this travel journal as well as the Peru journal because my experiences were quite surreal when I was living them. Reading about my travels and experiences at a later time brings me back to a place that is so different from my life in the US. This makes me grateful for what I have and for what I have seen.

My travel journal was organized in order of the dates. I would write the itinerary before I even left on the trip and I would journal about what I thought was going to happen each day. I would plan days if there were no plans in the tour book.

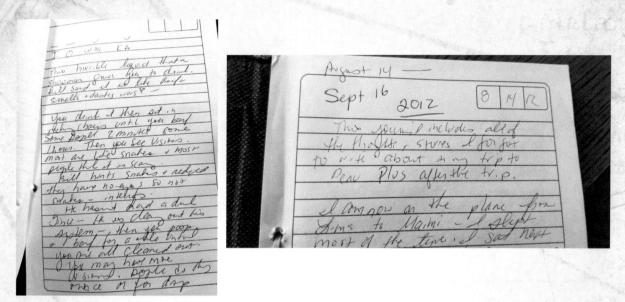

The first picture of the journal is my Cuba journal. I bought it before I went to Cuba because I knew it would be an adventure of a lifetime. Boy, was I right. It was such an adventure and not the kind that I had imagined. It was a cruise and we were supposed to…you guessed it! Cruise! But, the weather was not perfect so we had to dock and travel on a bus to our different "ports." The good news is that we did get to see another city that was not on our itinerary. The next set of pictures show a journal that I bought in Peru. I adore the fabric and leather. The llama carved into the leather is my favorite part of the cover. The other picture is about a person we met who tried ayahuasca. I wrote about a guy who took this magic potion from a shaman. They said it was a horrible tasting liquid that makes you vomit and get cleaned out from all orifices. A trusted person sits with you so you don't totally freak out when you start having "visions" (usually of snakes). I'm sure that I would never have remembered this interesting story if I had not written it down in my journal. In fact, I have gone back to this very page when my Peru traveling buddy can't remember the name of this magic drink. We heard many tales, both good and bad, of people imbibing on this dreaded or spiritual journey.

I know many people who keep a photo travel journal. When my parents travel all over the world they take pictures and put them on their computer screen show. That way they remember each photo. I knew one couple who made sort of scrap books from their travel adventures. They would insert the photo, then write a story to accompany the photo. These stories would form a narrative of their trip. I remember they kept these "journals" in white 4-inch, three-ring binders stacked on the top shelf of the bookshelf in their office. Each binder had a name for their trip; for example, Turkey, The Greek Islands, and Around the World Cruise. There are many different forms of travel journals.

Can you think of a place that you wish to visit? Are you planning a trip soon? Which kind of travel journal is for you?

I would use a travel journal   I would not use a travel journal

Notes:

QUOTES JOURNAL

A quotes journal is a collection of quotations. These can be quotations by famous people, any person, or you! The reason people keep what I call "collections" journals, is because they love quotes and wish to have them available. Or they hear a quotation and decide they love it and wish to remember it or they said something astounding and want to record it.

I have always had a love for quotes. I used to look up a famous quote each day and post it outside my dorm room door on a dry erase board when I was in college. I did this when I worked in different offices. Recently, while working from home I started writing my own quotes on a small white board to inspire myself when I am working at my desk. I started writing them and erasing them each day. Now, I write them and keep a small journal on my desk to record each quote for each day. Maybe one day I'll write a book of my original inspirational quotes.

My business coach, Sheri, says the most inspirational things on our coaching calls. I always take notes so I can come back later in case I forget her words of wisdom. As she said something inspiring, I would write it in my notes. Sheri's virtual group coaching mastermind lasted for eight months with a final in-person session in Portland, Oregon. I was working and could not make the final session, so I decided to put together a list of her quotes that had inspired me. I put the 60 quotes in a slide show with original photos from one of the other group members and myself. The title of the masterpiece was "S.H.I.T.* Sherri says" (Spectacular, Helpful, Inspirational, Things). We got rave reviews from all who were at the event. I was so happy that I took great notes, and that she shares such inspirational reflections.

As I coach, I was inspired by one of my clients who has a way with words. I always took notes during our sessions and after our first round of coaching I went back through my notes and circled words and phrases he said that inspired me. I created a similar presentation to Sheri's presentation and sent it to him as a gift for being my coaching client. He was amazed that he had actually said all of those inspiring words. He also gained more confidence in his writing skills and his creativity. This presentation of his words (on photos) was a beautiful way to show instead of tell him that he

Quotes journal page

39

has great talent for writing inspirational works. As the saying goes, "A picture paints a thousand words." These were HIS words instead of my words. Much more powerful.

Other people use quotes journals for many reasons. I ran across a fellow Toastmaster who writes down things that people say, or quotations he's heard. His journal inspires him to write more detailed speeches. Toastmasters must give a number of speeches each year, but can sometimes have a creative block as to what they would like to talk about. Because Bob had this quotations journal, he always had something to talk about and an unlimited supply of speech topics.

Cubicles in offices are never private. I remember walking by a computer in a cube and each week there was a new quote, as the screen saver, scrolling by. These were quotes by famous people. I think the person who put the quotes up had a book of quotes or got a new one from the internet each week. So you can see that there are different styles of quotes journals.

Are you intrigued, inspired by, or interested in quotations? Do you know someone who often pontificates inspirational messages? Do you have a tendency to say the perfect phrase at just the right time? Would you be interested in keeping a quotes journal?

I would use a quotes journal   I would not use a quotes journal

Notes:

WINE JOURNAL

A wine journal is used to document different varieties of wines. One can document the wine with a photo or a description. Most people describe the taste of the wine. For example, "this Chardonnay from Napa Valley has a rich butter taste that ends with a touch of oak." There is an entire list of descriptors of wine[1].

Karl keeps a wine journal to document each wine he drinks. His journal is on his computer in a Word document. He takes a picture of the wine, then drinks the bottle and documents his thoughts about the wine. He also writes what type of food he ate with the wine and the occasion. My hardworking friend Michelle had a second job selling wines and educating drinkers about pairings with food. I had her host a wine pairing party for me and learned that wine really does taste different when paired with the proper food. For example, I tasted a heavy cabernet and did not like it until I paired it with dark chocolate.

I love wine but have never started a wine journal. I save corks from bottles that I drink with friends, and then collect them in a glass bowl located in the entryway to my house. It is a great conversation starter. We sign and date the cork, then make a wish and toss the cork into the bowl. This is great fun at parties or with your special someone. When my husband and I were dating he brought a bottle of wine to my house because I said I would cook dinner for him. When we opened the wine I took the cork and a magic marker and told him to sign his name and the date. Then I took him to the big glass bowl and told him to make a wish – all the wishes come true. I had no idea how romantic this gesture could be with the right person. He made a wish and, four years later it came true (we got married). Now, I realize that this is not a journal per se, it is a collection, but it does journal the dates that various people shared wine with me. I remember one day my friend Beth looked through the glass bowl and we realized that we had drunk way too many bottles of wine together!

Wine Cork Bowl

Jeff Toister, my good friend and colleague, writes a wine blog called "Share The Bottle[2]." He and his wife, Sally, live in San Diego but often visit Napa Valley and other wineries. He shares his experiences, tastings, and awe-inspiring wines with his readers. He usually takes a picture of the wine and offers information about wine and hopes for comments. One of the best ideas I got about enjoying wine, I found on Jeff's wine blog: "Quick trick — whenever we receive a bottle of wine as a gift, we write the name of the person on the bottle with a silver marker. This way, we'll remember who to toast when we enjoy it." I had dinner with Jeff and Sally in May of 2018 and we drank a light rose' outside on their patio overlooking a valley. I still have the cork dated and initialed by all who were there. It is in my cork bowl! I still have the cork dated and initialed by all who were there. It is in my cork bowl!

Do you enjoy wine? Do you wish to remember what wines you like and which ones you don't? Would you like to document stories about who you drank wine with and the occasion? Is a wine journal for you?

I would use wine journal   I would not use a wine journal

Notes:

AUTOMATIC /INTUITIVE WRITING JOURNAL

Automatic or intuitive writing happens when the the writer lets a "force" channel words onto the paper. While researching this type of journal I found that most surrealist writers use automatic writing[1], which is defined as "leaving free field in the brain, writing every spontaneous thought down on paper before logic takes over and rephrases it." Picasso used **automatic writing**, hoping to release thoughts and images that might form the basis of his art. Mary, one of my first friends in Florida, took me to an automatic writing class where we were lectured on how to channel "the other side" and write our messages. I was not very impressed with the instruction or the class, but I was intrigued by the topic and the number of journals the instructor had completed. Days later I told another friend about the class and she told me about a woman who does this form of writing and is amazing. I had the opportunity to interview her and I learned so much about what she calls intuitive writing.

Kelli Lynne Poppe-Havel is an intuitive writer. According to Kelli, this is the process of creating an intention to speak to the highest forms of divinity possible, then writing what she hears in her mind. She is aware of what is around her and she does not leave her body, but she has no idea what she is writing. She shines her light out to the world like a beacon (illumination); her light shines on someone else, and what is reflected back is someone else's own light. It is almost like her light is a mirror, reflecting light back to another. She describes this as her higher self talking to another person's higher self. It is a message that comes from source, "from them for them" and "from themselves to themselves" when connected to the higher self. She sweetly calls them, "Love letters to yourself." She told me that she channels and writes the words of masters, Jesus, angels, unicorns, fairies, animals, trees, bodies of water, flowers, and nature.

Kelli Lynne
Poppe-Havel

She started intuitive writing when she was in first grade and learned how to write. She would write about her friends, Mr. and Mrs. Hicklebob, who lived in the attic of her house where she grew up in Kansas. She did this writing all of her life and only stopped when she went to college. In college, she wrote a paper on Mozart. Her professor commented, "This is a brilliantly written piece of work if it is all your own." She thought, "of course I wrote it – I don't cheat." But, she realized that she was channeling Mozart and he actually said it and she wrote what was he was saying to her. She admitted that the paper wrote itself. She stopped channeling and writing intuitively at that time and graduated with a BA in Communication using her own thoughts, research, and writing. She did not realize that this was called channeling until she went on a retreat in 2015 and was put in a situation where other people who channel could watch her. She then realized what she was doing and what it was called; she now writes messages from various sources who want to communicate with her. She also writes for people who ask her for a message from their higher self or guides.

I asked her to write for me and she got her beautiful butterfly stationery and an envelope, told me to relax and close my eyes and she began writing. I opened my eyes to watch her write. It seemed like she was writing a letter; she did not even notice when I went to check my phone or sat up and opened my eyes. When she finished, I read the letter. I asked her if she writes like this normally. She laughed and said, no she can't write that well.

Kelli's many past journals

Kelli recently moved to Florida and started writing intuitively as often as possible. She has many journals filled with letters and information from Jesus, Mozart, Archangel Raphael, and many sources. When Kelli was at Tracey Mahan's[1], a psychic and hypnotist, retreat, she was told that many on the other side are lining up because they want to be heard. She also draws what she is told to draw. Her journals are filled with writings, drawings, and highlighting. She said that she also writes in color because each guide or higher self has a color that means something to each person. One of her journals was written in a bright pink ink. Another was highlighted in yellow. Most of her journals are written in black ink. Sometimes she will take her written words and type them for her clients. She has a binder filled with typed messages.

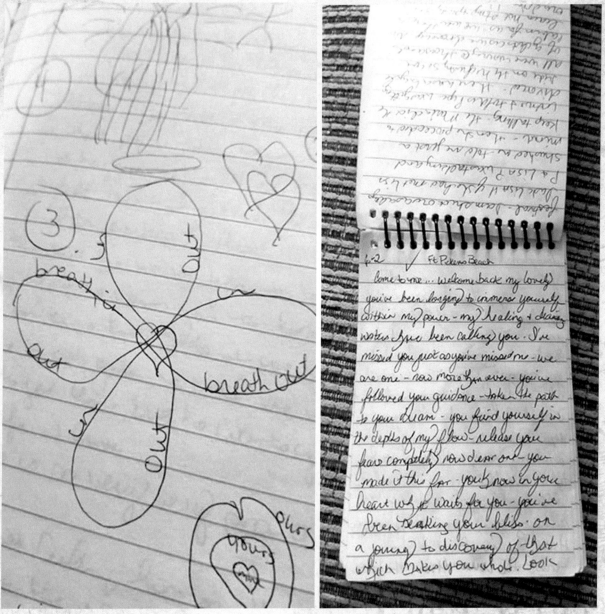

Kelli uses
drawings

Kelli's sample
writing

When I asked her if I can include one or two of her writing in my book she told me "Yes." She asked her guides what she should give me and was told that this is a universal message that comes from "source." This is an example of her intuitive writing channeled from a raccoon. Yes, one day she saw a raccoon and channeled this message.

Raccoon

April 21, 2017

Kelli writes in colors they choose for her

"I have come to you in this moment to facilitate the awareness which is derived from understanding the significance of lurking within the shadows; to illuminate you to the truth of duality. The truth that lies in the choice you make when you step into the outcome of a decision. I am that duality – I am a representation of dark and light – I am balance. I mirror the misconception of perception for I wear the mask of illusion. Not all is as it seems – some things are the perception of the mind in the event as it unfolds. When you allow the mind to control, you allow a window of reactive opportunity to get a stronghold on your response. You lose sight of the truth in that reality because you no longer lead with heartfelt intuitive guidance but rather you follow with instantaneous fear-based reaction. Your eyes of illumination are veiled behind a mask of distortion. Focus your imagery on my face — the face of raccoon. What is seen is what is presented - the image of one thing concealing another. To see only the outer dark shadows is to not see the light within. The light that emanates from the eyes; the outer dark shadows is to not see the light within. The light that emanates from the eyes; that light the outer dark shadows is to not see the light within. The light that emanates from the eyes; that light which IS the essence of the truth of your being. Until you gaze into the inner being, the outer projection takes precedence. See what is in front of you with the freedom that comes with knowing you are not what the mask represents; you are not what the mask hides when you are allowing yourself to be diminished. Seeing the world and seeing others in the darkness of the night is seeing yourself as a being with no light; a being with no divine spark; a lost being. Being in this darkness means allowing for the suppression of your light. This contrast is created to awaken you to the realization that there is a choice for you — a choice to remain hidden or to be magnified. Neither choice can or must be made on an intellectual level of thought; they were designed to be experienced to be felt with a mindful intention of an emotional outcome. What shall you choose? How will you respond? Does your heart reflect the shadows of illusion or does it illuminate the light of truth? What are you putting out into the world? All you are is all you share—with others and with yourself. Your mask is your safety net; the comfort that lies within the familiar; therefore, you allow fear to get its grip into your spirit. Because of your perception that there is a sense of solace and respite in the familiar, you have stifled the stirrings that would tell you otherwise. Remove our mask in recognition that the mask is what you believe others want for you rather than what it is you know you want from yourself — for yourself. Not a single self-destructive, self-deprecating, self-limiting belief you have is of or from another — it is that which is from self. Set yourself free. When you are free from yourself, you are free — free to be authentic, free to be magnificent, free to be you. I ask you now to let go of all the illusions; remove all your masks; and let go of those situations people, beliefs and habits that are not a part of the core being that you are. Seek guidance and gain confidence through the realization that nothing is ever as it seems; including yourself, until you step out of the distorted mask of illusion into the authenticity of truth. Accept the gifts that are being offered to you by the universe; accept the strength, power, courage, wisdom, peace and unconditional love that is given…that is within. Accept the truth. You HAVE everything you need; you ARE everything you need – you are complete; you are whole."

Do you have the ability to channel and wish to write down the thoughts of another? Do you wish to try this interesting way of using a journal? Would you be willing to take a class on automatic writing and using a journal to capture your messages?

I would use an intuitive writing journal   I would not use intuitive writing journal

Notes:

SEX JOURNAL

A sex journal documents aspects of sexual encounters. Included in the journal would be the date, other person's name, and a description of what happened. The main focus would be on what happened during sex and reflections after the act.

Cosmopolitan is filled with articles about sex, with titles such as "What his likes in bed reveal about his personality" and "Six ways to make him feel good." I never paid much attention to the magazine until the title "Hot SEX Diaries" (December 2017) jumped out at me as I stood in line to pay for my groceries. I bought the publication only for that article. I was intrigued not by the title but because it was a category of journal or so I thought. When I turned to the page expecting a detailed sex story from one person, I realized that it was just a compilation of sex stories from different people. I decided it was yet another way to sell magazines. It worked on me!

I never had a specific "sex journal" but I would write about making love to my husband, and when I was single, my boyfriends, in my regular journal because it was part of my journey. I did not get too specific about the physical part but wrote about my feelings. I would write about my day and if it ended with me and my boyfriend drinking wine on deck, then making love outside – that was included in my journal. When I first met my husband I wrote about all of our dates and when we finally had sex for the first time – yes – that was included in my journal. I noticed that sex is usually very frequent at the beginning of a relationship. The newness is exciting, so I wrote all about my desire to be with this man and no other man. The sex part was simply part of my day and night; I did not even think about having a separate journal to describe my sexual experiences.

I wondered if people kept journals exclusively to document their sexual escapades. One day, I mentioned that I was writing a book on journaling to Lisa. She told me that she started a special journal to document her newfound other part of herself; her sexual self. I am so happy that Lisa shared her journals and stories with me and let me read and write about her experience with what she calls her SEX Book. Lisa told me that she was in a pretty much sexless marriage for almost 15 years and, when she was suddenly single she had many adventures. After meeting and bedding several younger men, she decided to start writing about her single sex journey. She said she would like to read it when she was older, maybe married again, to look back and remember her explorations. She said this journal is only for her and she relives her exploits when she writes in her journal; that she feels alive during sex and loves to relive that feeling of freedom, empowerment, and connection. Here is a sample from her journal.

When editing this book, I decided that Lisa's example was too graphic to add. I did not want someone to buy this book and give it to their 13-year-old granddaughter without knowing this was in the book. So, for those of you who would like to read Lisa's sex journal example, I invite you to email me at LAR@LARG.com and I will email the story to you. *Please make sure to write "Lisa's Journal" in the subject line.* Thank you for understanding. Also, thank you to my editors for your sage advice.

Do you have sexual adventures that you want to remember or relive? Do you wish to try this unique way of using a journal?

I would use a sex journal   I would not use a sex journal

Notes:

LOVE JOURNAL

Journals documenting love from one person to another can be so very personal. There are journals from a wife to her husband, husband to his wife; mother to her child, sister to her sister, brother to brother or for your favorite grandparent, aunt, uncle or cousin. The journal can also be about the first few years of your child's life. The journal of our love can detail stories, adventures, and precious moments that your love can treasure for years. This is such a special gift because the stories are in your own words and come from your heart. They are written as no one else in this world can write emotions, feeling, and qualities of your special times together. You can give this journal as a gift or keep it for yourself to treasure the priceless moments in your lives.

I've kept this style of journal a few times. When I was 28 years old I met my first husband on a blind date. One of my friends set us up because we lived near each other and both had no family in the Washington, DC, area. I remembered she told me, "If I was not already married, I would marry him myself." That was a pretty good reference. He was perfect. We fell in love quickly and were talking marriage after about a month of dating. I had never been married before and was not sure if the bride gives the groom a present, but I decided that I would keep a journal of our dates and experiences together and give it to him as a wedding gift. It was a very small, lined, hardback book with a blue cover. I remember that I wrapped it in silver and white wedding paper and gave it to him the evening before we were to be married. He thanked me but I am not sure that he even read it. I know it sat on the table next to his bed for a while, then it disappeared. After our divorce, I am not sure that I remember packing it. But, as they say, it's the thought that counts.

I tried this again when I met Angel who I decided to date exclusively. I wanted us to get to know each other quickly because our relationship was moving quickly (are we detecting a theme here?). I bought a sexy little red book called, "All About US[1]." It is a journal of sorts. The author Philipp Keel wrote this book with a sense of adventure and fun. The book begins with a warm up of nonthreatening questions like; your names, dates of birth, and astrological signs. It gives A and B choices so one person in the couple chooses to make all of his or her answers A and the other B. The questions are listed in chapters called Here and Now, Favorites, Time Off, Playtime, Neuroses, and Choices. Angel and I answered the questions together. Angel is not much of a reader and does not have a lot of patience for questions, but he wanted to spend time with me so he agreed to answer. I learned a lot about him and his life by the way he answered the questions.

When it was Angel's turn to write, I realized that he has much better handwriting than I do (embarrassing). We did not finish the entire book…yet. Angel is now my husband and we have our entire future together to finish! This is the only journal that I have found where people write in a journal together. I suppose that any journal could be written by many people. This was an entirely new experience and idea in journaling for me.

All About US journal

Do you have a person who you love in your life? Do you think you would benefit and feel good writing about your journey in life or personal moments together? Are you hoping to find a present that is priceless to give to your special someone? Do you wish to get to know someone better and have a list of times you spent together during a special time? The Love Journal may be the perfect journal or the perfect gift.

I would use love journal   I would not use a love journal

Notes:

ART JOURNAL

An art journal is a place to create art and document your reflections. An art journal is different from a writing journal. Instead of writing, one draws or writes and draws. Amy Johnson Maricle, an expert at art journaling, writes on her blog[1] that "An art journal is the same as a written journal, except that it incorporates colors, images, patterns, and other materials. Several art journals have a lot of writing, while others are purely filled with images. It's a form of creative self-care."

I had never thought of an art journal as a practice until I was reflecting in my journal and started drawing because I could not describe my idea with words. As I drew, my niece Alyssa Gilbert came to my mind. Alyssa has been an artist all of her life. She has many sketchbooks and I asked her how many "art journals" she has. She told me that they aren't journals, only sketch books; then she showed me her collection. I realized that she has all of her books from when she first started drawing. She showed me her earlier books and then the later books. There is a huge difference in the journals. I could see that she had improved her drawings as time went on and each book was started. I asked her if she dated her artworks. She told me she did not date her drawings, but she knew which journals were older and which were newer.

Alyssa's self portrait

A box of art journals

Then I researched art journaling and discovered that it is a real practice. There are experts in art journaling. Amy Johnson Maricle's website www. mindfulartstudio.com is a valuable source of information about how to start an art journal. She has written books about art journaling, such as *Starting your Art Journal*[2] and *Art Journaling for Anxiety: Dwelling in the Mystery*, and holds online classes. She also uses and teaches how to use art journal for healing stress and anxiety. I would guess that some people relax when they draw or create visually, which is similar to how I relax when I write. Drawing is a great way to express yourself without words and it is a creative way to unwind.

Art drawing journal

Dawn DeVries Sokol is another art journaling expert and has written many books, including *Doodle Journeys: A Fill-In Journal for Everyday Explorers*[3] and *1,000 Artist Journal Pages: Personal Pages and Inspirations*[4]. Dawn also has very helpful videos about how to get started art journaling[5]. It seems that art journaling is a visual representation of journaling.

The art journals that I see online are very colorful, unique, and inspiring. I instantly noticed the colorful journals as I was researching online. If you are a visual person and reflect through drawing, painting, or other forms of art, an art journal might be your way of journaling.

Are you a visual person? Do you love to draw or paint? Would you rather create a form of art instead of write in a journal? If so, an art journal may be for you.

I would use an art journal   I would not use an art journal

Notes:

HEALING JOURNAL

There are many categories and formats for healing journals but generally a healing journal is best when someone has a health issue and wishes to write about his or her journey back into perfect health. This makes a lot of sense because having a health challenge can be stressful.

I know from experience that when I write in my journal when I am emotional, I feel less stressed. My journal lets me get my thoughts out of my head and on paper. Once the stressful thoughts are out of my head, I feel much better. Also, when I noodle, marinate, or reflect on a challenge in writing, I can visually "see" the answer much easier than if I only thought about the issue. Sometimes completely thinking about an issue makes it more stressful and the emotions seem to pour out, making matters worse. If I write, I can be emotional until all of the emotion is out on paper and then I can be more objective in solving my problem.

Swanwaters[1] is a company dedicated to helping survivors of abuse. Mags Thomson, one of the cofounders, has been writing in journals for years. She learned by experience that writing in a journal helped her heal from abuse. She and her team at Swanwaters are dedicated to helping others heal from abuse, and their blogs[2] are full of articles about how journaling can help in the healing process. Mags' free book, *Finding Your Wings: A Journaling Journey of Abuse Recovery*[3], documents how she used journaling in order to heal herself from abusive relationships. The book is also an excellent reference for journaling in general, as well as healing.

Beth Jocobs, Ph.D says in her book, *Writing for Emotional Balance: A Guided Journal to Help You Manage Overwhelming Emotions*[4], that, "Journaling can help balance and regulate your emotions." I have always found this to be true. One does not have to have a health issue to get health benefits from journaling. Writing about my feelings helps me to sort them out and think more clearly.

Do you have a health issue? Do you desire a healthier life? Are you stressed? Would a healing journal help you?

      I would use a healing journal   I would not use a healing journal

Notes:

MEDITATION JOURNAL

This journal is used after a meditation session to capture the wisdom gained from the practice. Having a meditation journal also lets you know your strengths and weaknesses during your mediation practice. For example, you can go back into your journal and discover that when you meditate at night you often fall asleep, but when you meditate after dinner you get wonderful visions and inspiration. Using dates on your meditation journal can help you go back and find themes in your meditation practices. For example, if you decided that during the month of May you had a difficult time concentrating because that May was a very stressful time in your life. On the other hand, if you were feeling stressed, you may find that the meditation helped relieve stress. The journal helps you write about your meditation experiences and track trends over time.

Gabrielle Bernstein wrote in her book, The Universe Has Your Back[1] about a type of meditation that inspires visions, and she suggested that you have a pen and paper available after the meditation. She suggested that the mediation is VERY powerful, so only think positive thoughts in the process. The directions are to sit comfortably for five to ten minutes in the energy of this creative mantra. You can listen to the mantra in your meditation and chant along (Ek Ong Kar Sat Gur Prasad Sat Gur Prasad Ek Ong Kar). You can download the mantra at GabbyBernstein. com/Universe[2]. When you are finished, open your eyes and start writing in your journal. At the top of the page write: "Thank you, inner wisdom, for writing through me. I invite the loving energy of the Universe to take over and lead me to a place of certainty." Next, read what you wrote down during the free flow ten-minute writing after the mediation. Allow yourself to be "inspired and vulnerable" by the images in the writing. Bernstein cautions that this does not always work; that it takes daily practice to connect and develop a relationship with the universe.

Next, I found a great example of a meditation journal as a blog on Donna Quesada's website[3]. This 10-day excerpt of the journal mentioned what was easy and what was difficult to do each day. It is a perfect example of writing about your meditation practice. I would always suggest to write what comes naturally to you. There is no right or wrong way to keep a meditation journal. Use it for what you wish; just remember to date your entries so you can go back and look for trends in order to improve your practice.

I started meditating years ago and continue to practice for at least 10 minutes every day. I sometimes use audio-guided meditations when I have time and a quiet place. Other times, I get quiet and focus on my breathing and try not to think. When I do get a thought (and I sure do), I pretend the thought is a bubble and I pop it to let it go. I quiet my mind. I find that meditation has helped me get calmer and has helped my "monkey-brain." Buddha wrote that monkey brain is when your brain won't stop spinning about thoughts. Kind of like controlling a bunch of crazy monkeys. According to *Guide to Buddhism A to Z*[4]: "The monkey mind (*kapicitta*) is a term used by the Buddha to describe the agitated, easily distracted and incessantly moving behaviour of ordinary human consciousness. Once he observed: 'Just as a monkey swinging through the trees grabs one branch and lets it go only to seize another, so too, that which is called thought, mind or consciousness arises and disappears continually both day and night'." Meditation was practiced because Buddha would rather have a mind like a "forest deer", always alert (not deer in the headlights).

I realized that I go through phases in my meditation practice. Sometimes I like to meditate in the morning outside on my lanai. Other times, I use guided meditation when I am looking for something specific, like healing or energy or specific affirmations. I do not have a book that I use for my meditation journal. I use online bookmarks because I usually use guided meditations on my iPad. The bookmarks and history act as a journal to let me know which meditations I practice and the dates. I realized recently that I had not used the guided meditations for about a month because I was traveling and meditated on the plane. That helped me relax and be refreshed when I landed.

Do you meditate? Would you benefit from using a meditation journal in your practice? Do you wish to start a meditation practice and want to document your progress?

I would use a meditation journal   I would not use a meditation journal

Notes:

MINDFULNESS WRITING MEDITATION JOURNAL

A mindfulness writing meditation journal is a journal where instead of meditation quietly to yourself, you would write your meditations in a journal for ten minutes or more. If you already wrote the entire mediation you would simply start over writing the same meditation over and over. The act of writing constantly becomes a form of mediation. Charles A. Francis, founder of the Mindfulness Meditation Institute, says about meditation journaling, "After a few days, notice how your thinking and behavior are changing. It's important to do the exercise consistently. The practice is most effective if it's done every day for several months, along with the mindfulness meditation practice."

Years ago when we thought about meditation we would visualize silent monks sitting on little pillows in the lotus position. Now, meditation is talked about in the mainstream as a way to calm stress and even connect with your higher self on other planes of existence (the universe). Even corporate giants have meditation rooms and give employees time and space to meditate. Google even has a course called "Search inside Yourself[1]," that was later made into a book by Chade-Meng Tan. The book is filled with exercises to help employees at work and in their lives.

One of the examples of a meditation journal is a loving-kindness meditation. The benefit of this meditation is to help you become more compassionate in your relationships. In this practice, you would write from your point of view about yourself, for example:

"May I be healthy and strong. May I be safe and protected. May I be peaceful and free from mental, emotional, and physical suffering. May I be happy and joyful. May I be patient and understanding. May I be loving, kind, compassionate, and gentle in my ways. May I be courageous in dealing with difficulties, and always meet with success. May I be diligent and committed to my meditation practice, and to helping others along their spiritual path. May my True Nature shine through, and onto all beings I encounter."

Next, you would write the same paragraph but keep your family in mind (kind of a prayer for your family); next, write about your neighbors, neighborhood, city, country, world, and finally the universe. Each paragraph can be embellished upon for each of the populations specifically. The idea is to start by embracing love and kindness for yourself, then end with sending loving kindness to everything.

If you have practiced meditation but it is not for you, try a writing meditation journal. This way you can focus on writing and not meditating. It is another way to meditate.

I would use a writing meditation journal   I would not use a writing meditation journal

Notes:

AFFIRMATIONS JOURNAL

In this type of journal, you write affirmations that you need at the time. Each day we all face challenges and have doubts about our abilities. An affirmation is a phrase or sentence that you say to help you feel better and give you a positive thought instead of negative thought. The idea is that if we think more positive thoughts we will be more positive and, subconsciously, we will grow into our affirmation: thoughts are things.

When I think of affirmations I think of Louise Hay[1]. In my mind she is the queen of affirmations. Her website has many general and specific affirmations. You can even get an email with an affirmation every day. She has written and published books (Hay House Publishing[2]) about affirmations and even suggests that if you use affirmations they can heal your life[3].

A few examples of affirmations are:
"I am beautiful"
"I am a successful businesswoman"
"I am confident in my ability to help others"
"I am financially savvy"

Notice that all of the affirmations start with the words "I am." It has been said that these two words are the most powerful words in the English language because what you put after them shapes your future. (Personalgrowth.com[4])

It is important to read your journal and your affirmations. I find that most people do not go back to their journal and re-read their affirmations. People tend to write affirmations in a book or journal, and then forget about them. As a coach, I suggest that you use affirmations and put them where you see them most often, for example, a mirror in the bathroom. That way you notice the declarations as soon as you wake up and go to sleep. This is not a journal but your favorite affirmations from your journal in plain sight each day. Do you face challenges and want a boost to your day? Do you want to shape your future? Do you already write affirmations?

I would use an affirmations journal   I would not use an affirmations journal

Notes:

WRITER'S JOURNAL

A writer's journal is a place where writers will write their thoughts and ideas for books or for a particular book they are in the process of writing. Kendra Levin wrote in an article on the webpage writersdigest.com[1] about ways to keep a writer's journal. She suggested:

- Keep a journal each time you sit down to write

- Ask yourself questions each day for five years

- Create a sentence about your day; combine that week into a poem

- Free associate any words that come into your head each day

- Choose only one moment each day to write about in full detail using all of your senses

According to author Doreen Virtue[2], do not use an audio recorder because you will never go back and listen to it. Actually, write your ideas in a book or online, then go back and break the ideas down into chapters. This works for her when she writes books.

I started a Word document on my computer when I had the idea for this book. Every time I had a thought about this book, I would write it in the Word document. I listed various categories of journals. When I started I had a list of ten then realized as time went on that there were more and more. I kept this list in my "writer's journal" before I began writing the book and added to it until the day it was complete. This journal helped me keep track of how many journals I was going to feature in this book and if I was going to write about any other topics regarding journaling. It began as notes and ended up being an outline of sorts. I did not use dates but wish I had so I could see my progress.

Are you a writer? Do you need more discipline or an outline form to assist you in your writing? Would a writer's journal work for you?

     I would use a writer's journal   I would not use a writer's journal

Notes:

LETTERS JOURNAL

A letters journal is a place where you can write letters to someone but you never send them. The act of writing the letters is cathartic. If the person has died and you cannot talk to him or her any longer, this is used instead of talking. Sometimes, you can hear thoughts in your head or that person's answer as you reflect on what you are writing. You can also write letters to people who are alive but never send the letters. Simply, the act of writing the letter helps clarify your thoughts or solves a problem.

I have written letters in my regular journal but never had a journal specifically for writing letters. I write letters and never send them because I can't take back what I say and I especially cannot take back what is in writing. I wrote these letters that I will never send because sometimes it is therapeutic to write and feel the feelings just to get them out of my head. Then I let it go. For example, I wrote a forgiveness letter to a person for what I perceived he "did" to me. In the letter, I described the situation, his actions, what effect it had on me and how I felt. Then, I forgave him stating, "I forgive you. You did what you thought was best for you at the time. This was what you knew how to do." I felt so much better after writing that letter and I have a much better relationship with that person now. Next, I wrote a letter stating my anger to a former friend. I knew that I was never going to send this letter so I only wrote what I was feeling. I don't know many nasty words but, believe me, all of the ones that I do know were in that letter. I cried as I wrote because I was never going to have a relationship with this person ever again. I was sad, angry, frustrated, and a bit mad. I could write directly without mincing words or sugar-coating my thoughts or feelings. I wrote and did not think about hurt feelings. After I wrote this letter I felt exhausted, cried out, but lighter. I let go of my anger – I got it out on paper and out of my head and soul. People may write letters, but then burn them to symbolize that they let whatever is troubling them go.

People have written letters to their children before their children could read. The idea of this kind of journal is to document what you were thinking when you were pregnant, delivering, and the years of your child's life. You could keep this journal for yourself or give it as a gift when your child graduates from high school or college or gets married.

My best friend, Carol Powers, has a letter journal. Carol was adopted and her parents loved her more than any parents could. She has told me stories of how her parents were strict and she was so independent. When she was a teen, she was an only child and loved to hang out with her friends. She broke curfew many times and was restricted and disciplined. But, even though she was challenging, they were always so proud of her. Carol's parents were older than most of her friends' parents and they died before Carol was 50 years old. Her father died sooner than she expected and she took care of her mother until she died seven years later. She misses them often and has a journal to write letters to them. Here is one of the letters she wrote to her parents in her journal.

"Dear Mom and Dad,

I have missed you so much today. This was always a special day for us because it was my adoption day! I am so blessed to have had you as parents. You taught me so much and loved me unconditionally. You were so strong in times of trouble, generous, and kind. How lucky I was to be chosen by you to be your child. I know that you are always here with me and that gives me strength. I will see you soon. I love you both."

She chose a pretty journal with flowers on it. Carol writes in her journal when she misses her parents and when she is lonely.

Example of letters journal entry

Write letters to your future self. My son's teacher in high school had the class write letters to their future selves. She held them until they gradated. I was amazed at how accurately his dreams had turned into reality. He said that he would go to Europe, Germany in particular. He said that he would get into a college in another state. He said that he would be in the top 5% of his class. He was right on all accounts. I had no idea he had such big dreams and goals. He made them all come true.

Think about writing a letter to your future self. The New York Times has an online newsletter called Motherlode. One article, "A Letter to My Younger Self", by Lisa Belkin, gives very good examples of letters. Editor Ellyn Spragins wrote a book called *If I'd Known Then: Women in Their 20s and 30s Write Letters to Their Younger Selves (What I Know Now)*[1]. It is about women under forty who wrote letters to the girls they once were. This would be a helpful and self-awareness-type of journal. I could write letters to myself for each decade or stage of my life, after each romantic relationship or after failures. What form of letters journal are you interested in keeping? Would you write letters to friends, future children, your children, people who have died, or letters to yourself?

I would use a letters journal   I would not use a letters journal

Notes:

HOLIDAY JOURNAL

A holiday journal is a place to document your holiday experiences. These can be any holidays. You can choose a particular holiday like Halloween or Christmas or your birthday or use all of the holidays. To start the journal, note who was there on that holiday: Did you have visitors or was it your immediate family? Write about special events that occurred over this holiday. This is a great time to record stories that can be told years later at the same family gatherings. It is also a great memory that includes pictures of those who are no longer with you or people who were visiting at the time.

You can have a Halloween journal to record all of the photos and stories of your family during this fun day of costumes. Imagine going back through the journal when your child is now an adult. You would have fun sharing this book of exciting times, costumes, and fashion throughout the years.

Holidays can also be vacations. A friend of mine had gone to Rehoboth Beach since he was born. It would have been wonderful if his family had kept a journal of all of the years in that beach house. I went on vacations to this beach house and I was sure that it was haunted. Pots and pans would fall off of the wall in the kitchen and radios would turn on automatically (before we had automatic music). If my friend had kept a journal, he could look back at all of the fond memories of his family's adventures in that haunted beach house. I hear that the property was sold and the "cottage" was torn down, and a huge house was build on that and the adjoining property. The holiday journal would have been a piece of history.

I received a Christmas journal as a wedding present in 1992. The book has two pages to guide you to document your Christmas each year. It begins with the date and address of where you gathered that year. Next there is a place for a photo and asks who joined in the cheer. The book includes lines to document special events of the holiday season and memories of the past year. I then would tape my Christmas card/letter that I sent that year at the bottom of the second page. Various years I put photos in the card. I kept this journal from 1992 until 2008; then I stopped. I started again when I was remarried December 2017. I love this journal because on each page I can see pictures of my son growing up. I also see pictures of myself throughout the years. I still say that when I lived in Texas the style was big hair!

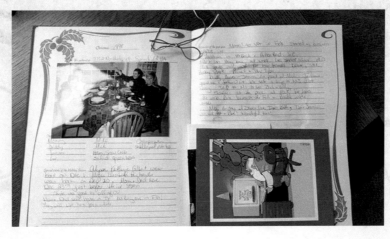

Holiday Journal example

Some of the entries that I documented are:

1992 – Mike's holiday party was at the Hard Rock Café. Since he is an FBI agent and we lived across the street from the FBI headquarters, it was a short walk! I won a silver bowl as a door prize. The Inaugural parade preparation is crazy.

1994 – We are living in my first house that is my house. I traveled to San Juan for work and loved Puerto Rico.

1995 – Christmas was in Plano, Texas, where we live now. Grandpa Wojcik is with us and mommy and daddy brought him down to spend time at our house. We got two chow chows, Jake and Alexis. I love my doggies.

1997 – Mick was born January 4, 1997. We were at Grandma and Grandpa's house in Iowa Park, Texas. I got laid off from my job in October but found out that we will be transferred back to DC in February. I am starting my own business!

1999 – Christmas at Grandma and Grandpa's house in Sun City Center, Florida. Best time was finding a conch shell on the beach. I gave it to Daddy but it still had an animal in it. He said after we left it was very stinky. Mick loved the all-you-can-eat snow crab legs that we had for Christmas Eve. I decided to dye my hair red for a holiday party (just a quick rinse) but it took a month to turn back to blond. We took a family picture and I have red hair. Crazy.

2001 – World Trade Center and Pentagon disaster. Many people in my neighborhood died. We had our playgroup ladies bring them dinners for three months. I went to NYC in January to visit Larry when he was working there. I walked and walked and took pictures of the World Trade Center site (ground zero). We went to Florida to see Grandma and Grandpa for Christmas. Mikki was with us and we went to Disney. Mick loved the train.

2003 – I got my Ph.D. We went to Germany for Janina's (2nd au pair) wedding. Mick held the candle. Mick is starting 1st grade in the German immersion program. We celebrated Christmas, New Year's and Mick's birthday in Florida with Grandma and Grandpa.

2005 –A card that says "We wish you a joyous New Year! Love Lori and Mick" with a beautiful photo of me and Mick dressed up for the holidays.

2017 – Angel David Garcia and I got married on the beach on December 27, 2017. I am starting this book again. There are only 8 more pages left. I am sure they will be full of great memories! Mick is a Junior at University of Miami. This year was wonderful in our new home in Sarasota, Florida. I love my life.

Do you enjoy holidays? Is there one special holiday for you? Do you love Halloween, Christmas, or your annual vacation? Would you especially enjoy keeping a holiday journal?

I would use a holiday journal   I would not use a holiday journal

Notes:

GOALS JOURNAL

A goals journal is a place to write your goals and document when they happen. American author Fitzhugh Dodson said: "Goals that are not written down are just dreams." Stop dreaming and start achieving your goals!

Athletes can have goals journals to document their achievements. The website writingathletes.com[1] is the best example of athletes writing their goals in a journal. Serena Williams, Michael Phelps, and Carlos Delgado all write their goals, feelings, and visions of greatness in journals.

Many goals journals come in the form of planners, such as the Panda Planner[2]. This planner can be used as a journal to set goals and break them into annual, monthly, weekly and daily tasks. Michael Leip, the founder and creator of Panda Planner says, "My hope with Panda Planner is that it will give you the motivation, the inspiration, the system—or whatever it is that you need—to set aside your stress and challenges, start living a fulfilling life, and crush your goals! Also, helping others become happier and more productive makes me happier and more motivated, sooooo....everyone wins! *High Five!*". I have a good friend, Blake, who loves these planners and told me about them because I was working on this book.

My goals journal is in my regular journal. I list my goals on the first page of each journal. Usually, on the first day of the New Year I will review my goals. I try to only have three to six goals because I realize if I have too many my thoughts are not focused on the goal. I am everywhere trying bits and pieces of everything. This year, I wrote my six goals, then categorized them. I created relationship goals, financial/business goals, travel goals, and weight loss goals. My process is that I take inventory of which goals I achieved and give myself credit, a smile, and a quick celebration. I look at the goals that I have yet to achieve and decide if I want to continue with these goals, re-think or re-write them, or get rid of them. I create S.M.A.R.T.[3] (specific, measurable, attainable, realistic, and timely) goals, a description of the goal, and also visualize my goal. If I can, I break them down into smaller tasks and give myself credit for doing these tasks to get me to my final goal.

I love the process of setting aside time each New Year to think about what I achieved the previous year and what I wish to achieve this year. I take time to think about my goals and write them as a sentence; then I give them more detail and description. Each time I open my journal I make sure to read the first

Lori's 1991 Goals list

page where my goals are listed. I believe that the more often I read my goals, the more time I will take to focus on their outcome. I've been setting goals most of my life in one form or another using my journal.

In 1991 I had a list of 5 goals. These goals were not SMART goals. At that time, I did not know how to write "smart" goals. I called it "What I want"

My 5 Goals

What I will achieve this year

1. Happy with my job – either stay with CS or find a more goal oriented job – work in training field – not just human resources
2. Help others – PG, Teach Aerobics
3. Finances – paid off 3 credit cards!!!
4. Man – relationship - √
5. My body

The next few pages of this 1991 journal details a long example and vision of what I meant for each goal. I wrote at least a page describing what I mean by happy with job, help/give to others, finances, man, and my body. As I look back I realize that I did change jobs that year. I started a job that changed my life; it moved me into the training and development field. Also, I helped others by teaching water aerobics and paid off three credit cards!!! It was also the year I met my first husband. And I realized the trend that I am always working on my body; either trying to get it into shape or keeping it in shape.

Do you have goals? Do you write your goals in a list somewhere and forget them or would you keep a goals journal?

I would use a goals journal   I would not use a goals journal

Notes:

MIRACLE JOURNAL

This journal documents evidence of miracles. The *Oxford Dictionary*[1] defines a miracle as "An extraordinary and welcome event that is not explicable by natural or scientific laws and is therefore attributed to a divine agency. Or a remarkable event or development that brings very welcome consequences." According to National Public Radio[2] citing a survey from the Pew Forum on Religion, over 80 percent of people believe in miracles.

The best description I have found for a miracle journal[3] is by Louix Dor Dempriey, the founder of The Louix Dor Dempriey Foundation[4], a non-profit educational organization dedicated to unconditional love that focuses on humanitarian projects. He writes on his webpage that "It is crucial to date and write down every Epiphany, Revelation, miracle, and lila (Divine play) that occurs in your life. Be sure to write your entries as close to their day of occurrence as possible. You do not have to retell the whole story, though you may if you wish. A line, phrase, or maybe even a paragraph is enough. If you keep a daily diary or journal, it is important to keep it separate from your Miracle Journal. In other words, it defeats the purpose and function of the Miracle Journal if you heap everything into it like you would a diary. Whereas a diary holds an account of everything in your life—emotions, happy and sad; your wins and losses, etc.—the Miracle Journal is an account of the miraculous, a single stream of powerfully positive thoughts and events… a consummation of love and transcendence. This unified field of love (the ultimate and only Reality) is what gives it its transforming power."

Anything that is extraordinary or remarkable that is not expected is a miracle. Keeping a journal of miracles gives us proof that wonderful things do happen in our lives. As I write this section, on a rainy day in May, I decided to take a break to walk my dog, Remmy. She is a very social dog and loves people more than she loves to do her business. And since it is raining I was hoping that she would be fast so I could get back to writing. Of course, when she saw my neighbor, Craig, pulling his car into his garage, she had to visit. Craig told me about his day sailing model boats with a group of sailing enthusiasts. They sail on Thursdays and Saturdays. I asked him if he sailed on this rainy day. He told me that for some reason there was a clearing in the clouds where they were sailing this morning. They sailed rain free for about two hours, then it started to drizzle and they packed it up. I was amazed. It had rained on and off all morning in our neighborhood. It was a miracle that they could sail today. This is an example of a miracle according to our definition (extraordinary and welcome event that is not explicable by natural or scientific laws and is therefore attributed to a divine agency). A miracle journal would document events similar to this one.

Lori Ann Roth Ph.D.

Miracle journals can also be tied to prayer journals. In my prayer journal I prayed that my friend Beth's father would be free of cancer. That seemed improbable and impossible because he had a rare form and was going through treatment that was hard on his body. I wrote the date that I started to pray in 2016, I wrote my prayer, and there was a blank spot for the answered column. Recently, Beth told me that her dad is doing great and he is cancer free. That is indeed a miracle! I then completed the prayer journal but also wrote this miracle in my miracle journal.

My miracle journal is separate and I don't keep it with my other journals. I keep it on a bookshelf in my office so that I see it every day and it reminds me that miracles do happen.

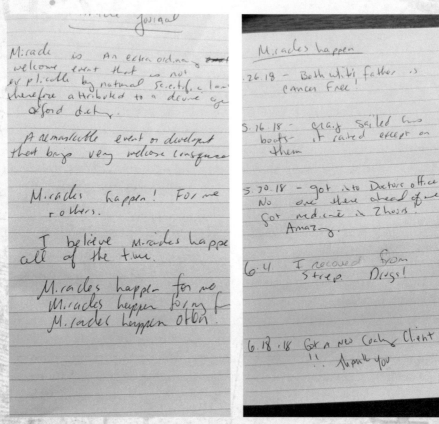

First page of Lori's Miracle journal   A page in Lori's Miracle journal

Another reason for a miracle journal would be re-reading it at a later time. Imagine a time that things are not going well in your life. You are sad or lonely. You just lost your job or a relationship that was

70

important to you. All is not well. Most of us have a tendency to start to feel sorry for ourselves. We cry or mope. Our mood becomes negative and gloomy. When I read my miracle journal after feeling down, I feel that hope is restored to my life. It brings me out of my gloom and I feel that another miracle can happen. I begin to look for small miracles and write about them. Soon the small miracles get larger and I am grateful and look forward to another day. I hope for more amazing miracles to make my life happier, better, and create a better sense of happiness.

Think about the miracles that have happened to you in your life. Think about the miracles that have happened around you, to your friends and family. Do you want to be amazed often? Do you want to keep track of the miracles on your journey? Will having a miracle journal help you when you are feeling down or negative about your life?

I would use a miracle journal   I would not use a miracle journal

Notes:

SPIRITUAL JOURNAL

A spiritual journal is a place to document your spiritual growth. This could be religious or only spiritual in the sense of counting your blessings or communicating with your higher self. A spiritual journal is different from a prayer journal because this type of journal documents your spiritual journey, whatever that means to you. It could mean finding your meaning in life, creating spiritual goals or reflecting on questions such as why am I here.

There are many kinds of spiritual journals, but most focus on the relationship between you and God, or whatever you call the force greater than humans. Some journals focus on reading a spiritual saying or passage and reflecting with words in a journal. I love this quote about journals and specifically a spiritual journal: "A journal is like a muscle: when you use it regularly, it can carry more spiritual weight in your life[1]." Dan K. Phillips[2] has a blog about his spiritual journey. It has a lot of information about connecting with God and being honest in your journal. There is also wonderful information about how to start a spiritual journal.

When I was in college I decided to read the Bible for inspiration and strength. My roommate at the time went to Bible studies and shared her knowledge with me. I would read the Bible, underline and highlight passages for understanding, then write my reflections in a journal. It was an educational journey and the process gave me something to think about. I learned more about history and I learned about myself. I used references to research about the Holy Land. I would go to the library (this was before the internet) and read books about locations that I read about in the Bible. I was inspired by the compassion of Jesus and reflected on my actions, thoughts, and behaviors. I am sure that I changed, grew, and became a better person because of this process. This journal lasted about two years, then I kept my regular journal and transferred my prayer journal into the back of my regular journal. I still keep a prayer journal and have also added a meditation journal.

Are you spiritual? Are you interested in reading the Bible or other religious writing and recording notes? Do you wish to record and document your spiritual journey through life?

I would use a spiritual journal   I would not use a spiritual journal

Notes:

BULLET JOURNAL

One of the newest types of journals is a bullet journal (BuJo). It looks like any other journal from the outside but the inside has a series of dots, similar to graph paper but only the dots all over the pages. Most people use the dots as a foundation to draw lines (using a ruler) or tables.

I first learned about this type of journal from an acquaintance of mine who says this is all the rage (my words not hers). She went on to say that many millennials are using them to plan and organize their way.

The bullet journal was created by Ryder Carroll[1], a digital product designer. Originally, Carroll designed the journal to deal with his attention deficit disorder (ADD) when he was a teen. The method of using this structured journal helped him focus and prioritize. When he shared his system with his friends, they were interested and he realized that it also works for people who do not have ADD as well.

The inside of a
bullet journal

Carroll created the web page www.bulletjournal.com and wrote a book, *The Bullet Journal Method*[2], to share his process with the world. He suggests the method will help you focus, adapt to help with challenges, stop overwhelm, and will declutter your mind. Bullet journaling answers the question, how do we use our energy and time? His main purpose for using the method is to help a person live a productive, more meaningful, and intentional life.

Ryder Carroll's method of bullet journaling consists of these items:

1. Index – first few pages of the journal
2. Future Log – an annual calendar
3. Monthly log – each month shown as a calendar and has a task list for each date
4. A Key – this is like a legend on a map.

   . (a dot) represents a task

   o (a circle) represents events

   - (a dash) represents notes

*(star) represents a priority

The journal can be used in this formal manner using the method Carroll created or it can be used for many other purposes. It can be used as a regular journal, a planner, to brainstorm, to keep track of tasks and events, and various other uses. There are many examples listed on Ryder Carroll's website under blog. There are many YouTube videos that describe how to use the journals in all types of ways. Some show a video "flip through" of a person's journal from previous year. They can also resemble art journals when the bullet journalist creatively uses pictures and drawings.

I realized that there is also a terminology for bullet journals. When the journalist completes a page or two pages side-by-side, it is called a "spread". When the creator shows each page to another person at one time, it is called a "flip through". There may be a "collection" where you "migrate" notes or you can use a key for "rapid logging". Ryder Carroll describes his method as an "analogue system" that takes time and dedication.

On her YouTube channel, creative bullet journalist, Amanda Rach Lee[3] talks about creating a "new spread." She also says that she admires "amazing spreads" that others have crafted. I have seen a flip through of her 2017 and 2018 journals as she documents her past journeys using video. Lee has a lovely way about describing how she has evolved in her journaling. She mentions what works for her, and what does not. She is not judgmental about other's journals; she describes what she has done, and what may work for you. Her journals are an amazing balance between a time management system and artful pictures and drawings. She even has videos depicting how to draw titles, flowers, and other useful or decorative illustrations.

Do you need some structure? Do you have too many priorities and need to focus? Would you like to make your own system to manage time? Are you willing to spend the time each day to record your schedule, tasks, and events? Do you wish to lead a more intentional life?

I would use a bullet journal   I would not use a bullet journal

Notes:

SOCIAL MEDIA

They say there is an app for everything. Yes, there are journaling apps, but there are many applications on social media that can be used as a journal. Many of us are addicted to social media and need to check how our friends are doing and post what we do. My son told me once that Facebook is for "old people" and the younger generations use other forms of social media, like Snapchat or Instagram. Some social media applications like Facebook never go away and others only show "posts" for mere seconds before the posts vanish. A few apps tell "stories" that are similar to mini journal entries. A handful simply list where you are and who you are with as well as showing a photo. There are many different styles of social media applications to choose from. Find one that you know you will use if this is your form of journaling. I've heard people say that these social media applications are not great because only the "good" times are posted. It is not a realistic documentation of your life. To that I say – so what? Post what you like and document what makes you happy. This is for your benefit and the benefit of your friends who matter. If someone does not like what you post he or she can "unfriend" you or simply not use the application.

I've had a Facebook account since June of 2009 and have posted at least once a month. Like most people, I post pictures of myself with other people, places I've been, or things that I've seen. Each entry is dated. This online semi-public journal is very visual and documents moments in my life and in my friends' lives too. I post pictures of sunsets, animals, birds, and strange events.

A group of my friends came up with a game on Facebook called "Real people or Show people?" They posted pictures of people they saw on the street or professionals doing strange things or not looking like an average person on the street. When I was in Denver for a conference I saw two young men with fantastic hair styles and posted for my friends to decide. They were real people but looked like show people. This game continued for years.

The relationship with my husband is documented on Facebook, with pictures and places where we've been. This is my first romantic relationship where Facebook documented our first date, vacations together, and milestones like graduation ceremonies, moving to a new state, birthdays, and our wedding. In fact, most of my friends discovered that we got married unexpectedly after we posted on Facebook. My husband used Facebook when we met, but is not a fan any longer because of the security issues. I still use it to post pictures, "catch up" with friends, and wish people a happy birthday.

The younger generation has grown up with social media and documents everything in their lives, from what they are presently thinking to what they had for breakfast (photo included). On Facebook, I've watched Julianna (JJ) Burke's[1] singing career grow from singing in a choir, to Grammy camp, and recordings online. I've watched her fan club flourish as she has matured into a beautiful young lady, both inside and out. Social media has documented a generation and changed how we keep journals.

I can go back through Facebook and remember the good times and laugh at the pictures. I can also see trends such as hair styles, fashion, and my weight gain/losses. If I have a question about who was at an event at a particular time, I can check back anytime. The problem is that once you have posted to social media it is forever.

Do you presently have a social media account that you use to document your life? Do you read friends' "journals" and posts? Have you gone back to a post to see what you looked like at that time or remember an event? Would you think about using social media as a journal?

I would use social media to journal   I would use social media to journal

Notes:

JOURNALING YOUR WAY

Now, it it your turn to start journaling. First, decide what type of journal you wish to keep. I would suggest a regular journal to start. But, feel free to begin any journal that gets you excited; a journal that you will be enthusiastic about using. Next, date your entry and write your ideas, thoughts, and emotions as the mood strikes you. Remember that it is very important to write the dates in your journals. This way it is easier to go back and find the entries and you can see results in your life.

Quick Survey

Now that you have read all of the types of journals it may be easy or not to decide which is best for you. If you are still having a challenge choosing a beginning journal let me help you with a short survey.

First, go back through the book and choose which journals that you said, "Yes, I would use this journal" or absolutely "No, I would not use this journal".

Type of Journal	I would use	
	YES	NO
Regular Journal		
Journal to Relax		
Prayer Journal		
Dream Journal		
Night Journal		
Possibilities/Intentions Journal		
Business – work journal		
Networking Journal		
Gratitude Journal		
Money Evidence Journal		
Travel Journal		
Quotes Journal		
Wine Journal		
Automatic /Intuitive Writing Journal		
Sex Journal		
Love Journal		
Art Journal		
Healing Journal		
Meditation Journal		
Mindfulness Writing Meditation Journal		
Affirmations Journal		
Writer's Journal		
Letters Journal		
Holiday Journal		
Goals Journal		
Miracle Journal		
Spiritual Journal		
Bullet Journal		
Social Media		

Next, see if there are any similarities in the types of journals that you chose. Were they goal oriented? Were they more creative in nature? Did they involve a hobby or interest of yours? If you have identified a certain type of journal, try one for a month or so then if you like it keep it; if not then try another in your type. If you are like me I liked a variety of types of journals. I started with the regular then kept adding different types. Some I did not keep, such as the dream journal; others I loved like the gratitude journal. My advice is not to choose too many. You don't want journal writing to be stressful.

Remember there are no strict rules. Be creative with your journal or not. Remember, it is YOUR journal. You can make it anything you wish it to be. There is no right or wrong way for you to journal. If you wish, no one will see your journal except you.

Thank you for reading this journal book. I wish you well on your journal journey. I hope that you go to my website and comment about the kinds of journals that you use. I would love to know if you started a journal because of this book, which journal you chose, and why. Please share at….www.larg.com.

ENDNOTES

Introduction

[1] https://www.authentichappiness.sas.upenn.edu/

[2] https://greatergood.berkeley.edu/profile/Robert_Emmons

[3] http://www.webmd.com/diet/news/20080708/keeping-food-diary-helps-lose-weight

[4] http://gladwell.com/outliers/the-10000-hour-rule/

[5] https://en.wikipedia.org/wiki/Marcus_Aurelius

[6] http://classics.mit.edu/Antoninus/meditations.html

[7] https://inbreathe.com.au/history-of-journaling/

[8] https://www.pepysdiary.com/

[9] http://www.bradshawfoundation.com/clottes/

[10] http://www.cslewis.com/us/books/?keyword=journal&bisac_heading=combined&order=relevance

[11] https://www.annefrank.org/en/

[12] https://en.wikipedia.org/wiki/Etty_Hillesum

[13] https://rarebooks.nd.edu/digital/civil_war/diaries_journals/index.shtml

[14] https://www.telegraph.co.uk/culture/art/art-features/10997667/The-secret-life-of-Frida-Kahlo.html

[15] http://www.openculture.com/2017/07/leonardo-da-vincis-visionary-notebooks-now-online-browse-570-digitized-pages.html

[16] http://www.oprah.com/spirit/oprahs-private-journals-diary-excerpts

[17] https://www.amazon.com/What-You-Think-None-Business/dp/051509479X

[18] https://theheartysoul.com/oprah-life-changed-journal/

[19] https://en.wikipedia.org/wiki/Emma_Watson

[20] http://www.rookiemag.com/2013/05/emma-watson-interview/

[21] http://www.thirteenvirtues.com/

[22] https://www.brainyquote.com/quotes/natalie_goldberg_499312

[23] https://www.lisashea.com/lisabase/journaling/basics/

Journal to Relax

[1] http://www.buddhisma2z.com/content.php?id=274

Prayer Journal

[1] http://www.smallgroupchurches.com/small-group-prayer-journal/

Dream Journal

[1] http://browseinside.harpercollins.ca/index.aspx?isbn13=9780007299041

[2] https://www.dreamscloud.com/en/dream-dictionary/symbol/flying

Night Journal

[1] https://healthguides.healthgrades.com/getting-a-good-nights-sleep/journaling-before-bed-can-help-ward-off-sleeplessness

Night Journal

[1] https://healthguides.healthgrades.com/getting-a-good-nights-sleep/journaling-before-bed-can-help-ward-off-sleeplessness

Possibilities/Intentions Journal

[1] https://www.imdb.com/title/tt0408985/

[2] https://www.thesecret.tv/products/the-secret-book/

Business – work journal

[1] https://www.forbes.com/sites/williamarruda/2013/10/22/the-one-thing-successful-people-do-every-day/#12daf2db7c6a

[2] https://hbr.org/2017/07the-more-senior-your-job-title-the-more-you-need-to-keep-a-journal

[3] https://www.skipprichard.com/why-journaling-makes-better-leaders/

[4] https://www.apa.org/pi/aids/resources/education/self-efficacy.aspx

[5] https://en.wikipedia.org/wiki/Mind_map

Networking journal

[1] https://zapier.com/learn/crm/best-crm-app/

Gratitude journal

[1] https://greatergood.berkeley.edu/profile/Robert_Emmons

[2] https://www.amazon.com/Thanks-Practicing-Gratitude-Make-Happier/dp/0547085737/ref=pd_lpo_sbs_14_img_0?_encoding=UTF8&psc=1&refRID=HPYK3SG0MBGX2EQNMM7S

[3] https://www.amazon.com/Gratitude-Works-Creating-Emotional-Prosperity-ebook/dp/B00BV8OYL6/ref=sr_1_1?ie=UTF8&qid=1529696654&sr=8-1&keywords=gratitude+works

Wine journal

[1] https://winefolly.com/tutorial/40-wine-descriptions/

[2] http://www.sharethebottle.com./

Automatic /Intuitive Writing journal

[1] http://www.surrealismart.org/history/writing-techniques.html

[2] http://traciemahan.com/

Love journal

[1] https://www.amazon.com/All-About-Us-Two-You/dp/0767905016/ref=sr_1_1?ie=UTF8&qid=1527448977&sr=8-1&keywords=all+about+us+book

Art journal

[1] https://mindfulartstudio.com/?doing_wp_cron=1546204628.3996450901031494140625

[2] https://mindfulartstudio.com/e-books/

[3] http://mindfulartstudio.com/art-journaling-for-anxiety-dwelling-in-the-mystery/

[4] https://www.amazon.com/Doodle-Journeys-Fill-Everyday-Explorersdp/1419728628?SubscriptionId=AKIAIOCEBIGP6NUBL47A&tag=&linkCode=xm2&camp=2025&creative=165953&creativeASIN=1419728628

https://www.amazon.com/000-Artist-Journal-Pages-Inspirations/dp/1592534120

[5] https://www.youtube.com/watch?v=eQXXNejnn5k&t=2s

Healing journal

[1] https://swanwaters.com/

[2] https://swanwaters.com/journaling-for-emotional-healing/

[3] https://www.amazon.com/gp/product/B071QX4TCL

[4] https://www.amazon.com/Writing-Emotional-Balance-Overwhelming-Emotions/dp/1572243821

Meditation journal

[1] https://www.amazon.com/s/?ie=UTF8&keywords=the+universe+has+your+back&tag=goo
ghydr-20&index=aps&hvadid=241922548046&hvpos=1t2&hvnetw=g&hvrand=173522604
32014045536&hvpone=&hvptwo=&hvqmt=e&hvdev=c&hvdvcmdl=&hvlocint=&hvlocphy
=9012311&hvtargid=aud-589036435099:kwd-192991940729&ref=pd_sl_69cjxxpzzx_e

[2] https://gabbybernstein.com/universe/

[3] https://donnaquesada.wordpress.com/2011/08/05/an-insightful-honest-10-day-meditation-journal/

[4] http://www.buddhisma2z.com/

Mindfulness Writing Meditation Journal

[1] https://www.barnesandnoble.com/p/search-inside-yourself-chade-meng-tan/1106580352/26886
35068121?st=PLA&sid=BNB_DRS_Core+Catch-All,+Low_00000000&2sid=Google_&sourceId=
PLGoP79700&gclid=EAIaIQobChMImLTc-Iq92gIVQgOGCh1z0AogEAYYAyABEgJ5x_D_BwE

Affirmations journal

[1] https://www.louisehay.com/

[2] https://www.hayhouse.com/

[3] https://www.hayhouse.com/you-can-heal-your-life-30th-anniversary-
edition?utm_source=LHcom&utm_medium=Blog&utm_campaign=LH.com_YCHYL

[4] https://www.personalgrowth.com/about/

Writers journal

[1] https://www.writersdigest.com/online-editor/5-new-ways-for-writers-to-keep-a-journal

[2] http://doreenvirtue.com/

Letters journal

[1] https://www.amazon.com/kindle-dbs/entity/author/B001IGUSQ6/ref=dbs_a_def_rwt_hsch_vu00_tkin_p1_i2

Goals journal

[1] http://www.writingathletes.com/whats-an-athletes-journal.html

[2] https://pandaplanner.com/

[3] https://en.wikipedia.org/wiki/SMART_criteria

Miracle journal

[1] https://en.oxforddictionaries.com/definition/miracle

[2] https://www.npr.org/templates/story/story.php?storyId=124007551

[3] http://www.louix.org/the-importance-of-keeping-a-miracle-journal/

[4] http://www.louix.org/about/the-foundation/

Spiritual journal

[1] http://www.spirithome.com/spiritual-journal.html

[2] http://edge.edge.net/~dphillip/Journal.html

Bullet journal

[1] https://bulletjournal

[2] The Bullet Journal Method, Ryder Carroll

[3] https://www.youtube.com/watch?v=aHnP7XGwFe8

Social Media

[1] https://www.facebook.com/motherradish

ABOUT THE AUTHOR

Lori Ann Roth, Ph.D., is the President of "Learning and…Reflective Growth," a company that specializes in training and coaching. She has dedicated her education, knowledge, and experience to enhance the personal and professional development of others.

Dr. Roth designs learning and facilitates training classes in leadership, customer service, and team building, as well as customized programming for specific needs. Through her coaching and training, she also enjoys helping individuals navigate transitions and learn life lessons, and maintains a busy schedule training and coaching clients across the country, including in Florida, New York, California, and Washington, DC.

Dr. Roth received her undergraduate degree in Psychology and Communication and a Master's degree in Adult Education from Michigan State University. She earned her PhD from Virginia Polytechnic Institute in Human Development. The emphasis of her doctoral studies focused on adult learning and human resources management. For over 35 years, Dr. Roth has worked in organizational development and training at universities, corporations, hi-tech companies, and small businesses.

She lives with her husband, Angel, and rescue dog, Remmy, in Bradenton, Florida. They are empty nesters but their children, Angelyanne and Mick, always have an open invitation to stay. Lori's favorite saying is "Be your best you!" She is an enthusiastic and avid journaler. The Journal Book: Your Journaling Journey is her first book.